AN ANGLO-IRISH HERITAGE

To all the ancestors

An Anglo-Irish Heritage

The Seward and Clarendon Families 1795 – 1955

Tony Seward

2019

Published by Independent Publishing Network

First published in the United Kingdom 2019

ISBN 978-1-78972-661-9

Please direct all book orders and enquiries to the author:

t.seward396@btinternet.com

Tony Seward
45 Victoria Road
Barnard Castle
County Durham
DL12 8HR
United Kingdom.

Typeset in Monotype Sabon
Designed and typeset by Belinda Magee

Printed and bound by Book Printing UK

Contents

Prologue vii

Seward and Clarendon family tree xii

1 **Industry and the Church:**
The Ewart and Clarendon Families 1790-1914 1
William Ewart and Son
Linen and Belfast
Sir William Ewart and his connections
Enter the Clarendons

2 **American Interlude:**
The Jones Family in Ireland and the USA 20
Family life and the professions in 19th century Ireland
America!
'The Witch of Staten Island'
Nina and Victor: courtship and marriage

3 **New York and Belfast 1911-1942** 47
The New York Years 1914–1924
Settled in Belfast 1924-1939
Growing up and school in Ireland
Love and war 1939-1942

4 **Seafaring, Emigration and Railways:**
The Seward Family 1795-1900 63
Prisoner of the French: John Rendell
Four generations
1. William Seward (d.1815), master mariner
2. William John Seward (1791-1858), master of an emigrants' depot
3. William Rendell Seward (1816-1884), railwayman
The emigrant's tale: (Samuel) Henry Rendel Seward (1824-?)
4. William Renell Seward (1845-?), engineer

5 Within Living Memory: The Sewards 1900-1946 87
Will and Grace 1900-1928
Grace, Dorothy and Bill 1928-1939
Love, war and marriage 1939-1942
A tale of three ships: *Saltarelo, Loosestrife, Inver*
The Home Front 1942-1946

6 Recovering Past Time: A Visit to 'Belhaven' 121
Aspect
Many rooms
Household management
Journey and arrival

7 Epilogue 131

Appendix 1: Seward family tree 134

Appendix 2: The British naval blockade and convoy system during the Napoleonic Wars 136

Appendix 3: VFC – the public man 137

References 141

Index 144

Prologue

What follows is the story of my family: the Anglo-Irish Clarendons , and the English Sewards. It is written in the belief that we should remember and celebrate our ancestors. As the steersman pictured on the title page relies on the stars – 'Si je les perds je suis perdu' (If I lose them I am lost) – so we too need some fixed reference points as we try to plot our own course through life.

The narrative covers the period from around 1800 to the mid-twentieth century. It relies largely on letters from family members living in England, Ireland, the USA, India and Australia, recounting their personal experiences of war with France, the linen business, the church, migration, seafaring, engineering and shipbuilding. It covers the rise and fall of manufacturing industry in Britain, two world wars and the period of my own early childhood, from 1943 to the early 1950s.

My starting point is three special objects currently in my possession, which, in their different ways, reflect the Irish, American and English strands in the history of the two families. The first is a silver salver bearing the following engraved text:

This Salver (part of a Service of Plate)
is presented to William Ewart, Jr. Esqr.
by his fellow townsmen
in recognition of his private worth as a citizen
and his public services as
Mayor of Belfast,
during the years 1859&1860
March, 1861.

[and on the reverse]
VICTOR FREDERICK CLARENDON C.B.E.
Grandson of WILLIAM EWART JR. 1817-1889
1st Baronet
gave this salver to his Daughter MAUREEN's son
ANTHONY WILLIAM RENELL SEWARD
being the eldest Great Great Grandson
of the salver's original owner
June 1959

The second object is a mourning sampler embroidered by a young American in 1838. Her name is Eliza Ann Bodine, but we do not know her age at the time, as she appears to have followed the common practice of unpicking it from the sampler in adulthood so that no-one would then be able to work out how old she was. She was probably about 10, as she was born c.1828. It depicts a tomb with an inscription beneath it commemorating her uncle, William Albert Housman. Surrounding this central motif are weeping willow trees, flowers and various consolatory texts, headed by a verse by Edward Young, from his long poem *Night Thoughts* (1742), while the others are from hymns. This American connection is explored in Chapter 2.

Smitten friends
Are angels sent on errands full of love
For us they languish, and for us they die.
Young.

Miss Eliza Ann Bodine's WORK
aged ... years
New York
1838
O Praise ye the Lord
Prepare your glad voice

His praise in the great
Assembly to sing
In our great creator
Let israel rejoice
And children of sion
Be glad in their king

Sacred to the Memory of
William Albert Housman
of Staten Island
State of New York
Who died November 1st 1834
Aged 22 years 10 months, & 10 days.

When blooming youth is snatched away
By death's resistless hand,
Our hearts the mournful tribute pay
Which pity must demand

Happy the child, whose tender years. Receive instruction well. Who hates the
sinner's path, and fears The road that leads to hell. Tis easier work if we begin
To fear the lord betimes. While sinners that grow old in sin. Are harden'd in
their crimes.

The final, English, item is a silver tankard presented to my grandfather by the Directors of Thornycroft's after the First World War, with an accompanying letter dated 9 April 1920. The tankard carries the following inscription:

[Engraving of Coastal Motor Boat (CMB) on lid]

Presented to
W.R.Seward Esqre.
by the Directors of John I. Thornycrofts & Co. Limited
as a token of their appreciation
of his work during the War
in organising the construction of
one hundred and fourteen CMBs
on the success of which the Admiralty
have expressed their congratulations and thanks.

The letter largely repeats this wording but also emphasises how

'Those not directly connected with the business can have little idea of the very great volume of work involved in dealing with so many Sub-contracting firms...'.

The stories behind these objects will emerge as the narrative unfolds. They immediately suggest a number of themes which will be explored: the central part played by the Ewart linen manufacturing dynasty within the Irish family network; the experience of migration to the USA (and in one case back again to Ireland); and the major part played by the sea, engineering and shipbuilding in the lives of the English Seward family. Our history will embrace the Industrial Revolution, the Church of Ireland, two world wars, the decline of manufacturing industry, and the beginning of the post-war transition to the modern world in the 1950s and 60s, as experienced by two families brought together in the 1940s by the chance of war.

My primary sources for what follows are hundreds of family letters, drawings, photographs and personal objects making up an extensive Clarendon – Jones – Seward collection, at present held at our house in Barnard Castle, Co. Durham. This was transformed from a mass of 'stuff', which ended up with me after the deaths of my grandparents and parents, into a well-ordered archive by my wife Angela. I am deeply grateful to her for the months of work she put in, sorting all the items into themed envelopes, and attempting to date them and identify the subjects of the photographs where these were not indicated. My grandmother Nina was meticulous (other relatives less so) about labelling her photos, but she very seldom included a date! Without Angela's contribution I doubt if I would ever have attempted to weave the contents of the archive into a coherent narrative: when I did it became a pleasure, as she had prepared the ground so well.

I have also drawn on the separate archive held by my sister-in-law Elizabeth Seward at her home in London, which is the main source for Chapter 4 on the early Sewards, 1795-1900. My brother Tim had made considerable progress on putting it into order and labelling it before he died in 2001, and his investigations resolved many grey areas and genealogical puzzles relating to the generations preceding my grandfather, William Thomas Renell Seward. His work has been invaluable in enabling me to balance the account of the Clarendons in the nineteenth century with that of the Sewards through the same period.

The Seward family tree (pp.134-5) has been prepared in some detail, as there is no other readily available source for the information contained on it. The situation for the Clarendons is somewhat different, in that various family members possess trees for their respective branches, and the authoritative Ewart family genealogy prepared by Wyclif McCready in 1929 gives comprehensive coverage of the Ewart and Clarendon families up to that date. I have therefore focused, in the tree for the Clarendons and Sewards (pp. xii-xiii), on the individuals referred to in the narrative – in effect, those in the direct line. This policy has inevitably resulted in the exclusion of some close relatives that I would ideally have wished to include, but it seemed the best way of clarifying the relationships in the story as written.

I am grateful to my former publishing colleague Ruth Taylor and cousin Nigel Blanchford whose comments on the draft enabled me to make significant improvements to it; also to my cousins, the children of Rev. Randal Clarendon – Sister Verity Anne, Lynette Morris, Owen Clarendon and Philippa Seldon – for sharing their detailed knowledge of the Clarendon family, and for the loan of key letters and photographs. Finally, special thanks must be reserved for my cousin Belinda Magee, whose enthusiasm and belief in the project has been a constant encouragement to me and whose design expertise was crucial in transforming the raw typescript into a handsome finished book.

We begin with the Irish story.

Tony Seward
Barnard Castle
November 2018

The Seward and Clarendon Families

William Seward, d.1815
master mariner
m.1790 Sarah Rendell, 1765-1843

William John, 1791-1858
Master of the Emigrants Depot, Plymouth
m. 4 times: (1) and (2) unknown
(3) Ann Rendell, d. 1830
(4) Mary Pike, d.1861

William Rendell, 1816-1884
station master
m. 1838 Charlotte Poe Renell,
1811-1897

William Renell, 1845-188?
railway engineer
m. Sarah ('Etta') Elliott, 1852-1938

Charlotte Cecilia Hadassah (Lottie)
1876-1963 m. Hubert BLANCHFORD, 1874-1960, *stained glass artist*

William Thomas Renell
1880-1928
engineer m. 1906
Grace Florence Edwards,
1886-1978

Ralph Renell
1883-1970 *engineer*
m. Wyn Cannon

Dorothy Grace
1909-1958 *journalist*
m. 1939 Thomas Robertson (Bob) KIDD, *businessman*, d.1983

John William
1947-

William Renell
1912-1966
engineer

m. 1942

Maureen Cecil
1915-2000

Anthony William Renell
1943-
m.1968 Angela Gail Wilmot,
1947-

Jennifer
b. and d. 1947

Miranda Caroline 1973-
m. 2002 Glenn HAYWARD, 1973-

Katherine Elizabeth 1977-
m. 2003 James McLEISH, 1974-

Oliver Andrew
2006-

Toby James
2009-

Emily Alice
2007-

Frederick Villiers Clarendon
1820-1904
architect and civil engineer
m. Margaret Jane Slacke

Thomas William
1855-1934;
Dean of Dromore and Rector of Maralin
m. 1879 Lavinia Ewart, 1853-1913

Dorothea Mary, 1880-1956;
m. 1915 Reginald WARD,
1877-1943

Rev. William Randal Slacke
1882-1956; m. 1931
Norah Barnet Steen,
1902-1997

Victor Frederick, CBE
1887-1972;
Chairman, William Ewart and Son Ltd
m. 1911 Nina Virginia Gregory
Jones, 1887-1968

Philip Randall Desmond, 1912-1985
Director, William Ewart and Son Ltd
m.1948 Eileen Craig, 1926-1982

Virginia Ewart, 1919-2001
m. 1952 Commander Brian
Scholes MAGEE, RN,
1906-1985

Belinda Jane, 1953-
m. 1982
Niall DOULL-CONNOLLY
(Connolly), 1951-

Timothy Clarendon
1949-2001
m. 1983 Elizabeth
Anne Debnam,1952-

Jeremy Philip
1953-1973

William Debnam
1983-

Ralph James
1988-

Daphne Virginia, 1949-
m. 1973
Patrick MEENAN, d.

Elizabeth Wendy, 1952-
m. 1974
John WYNN, 1952-

Victor Randall Ewart, 1958-
m. Carol Clarke, 1957-

Diana Louise, 1960-
m. (1) 1982
John HUGHES, 1955-
(2) Terence SKIPPER, 1957-

Compiled by Tony Seward, December 2018

1 Industry and the Church: The Ewart and Clarendon Families 1790–1914

William Ewart and Son

In around 1790, the first William Ewart (1759-1851) moved from Hillsborough in County Down to Balymacarrett, at that time a small settlement across the River Lagan to the east of Belfast's city centre. There he set up as a manufacturer, initially in the newly developing cotton industry. The enterprise prospered, and in 1814 he formed a partnership with his eldest son, William Ewart II (1789-1873). William Ewart III, who was to become the First Baronet, Mayor of Belfast, and an MP, was born in 1817.

According to *Grace's Guide to British Industrial History*[1], the firm did not diversify into flax until 1840, establishing its first mill, powered by water, in the Crumlin Road. However, the company's brief historical brochure, published in 1950 and revised in 1961[2], claims that 'The Ewart family began to make Irish linen in the latter part of the eighteenth century', and the *Dictionary of Ulster Biography*[3] records that the family business started with 'small-scale damask weaving'. What are we to make of this apparent discrepancy? It is possible that the Ewarts also acted as middlemen through this period, buying 'brown linen' from rural weavers and finishing it for sale to Britain and overseas (see below). By 1850, the transition from hand to power loom weaving had been completed, and in 1852, William Ewart and Son purchased the Glenbank bleaching works to the north of the city, thereby creating full vertical integration of the manufacturing process: from spinning, through weaving, to finishing of the cloth. My uncle Desmond, a Director of Ewart's, was for many years the manager of the Glenbank bleaching and dyeing works, living with his family in spacious Ballysillan House nearby.

Expansion continued through the remainder of the century. In 1859 the firm moved to extensive warehouses at 11 Donegall Place, although it kept the mills at Crumlin Road. From 1876 it began to acquire the assets of failing competitors such as the Bedford Street Weaving Company and Mountain Mill at Ligoniel, where it built 500 houses for its employees.

During the depression of the1880s, in order to protect the family wealth, the business was turned into a limited liability company, with a capital of £500,000. There were six partners: Sir William Ewart himself, and five sons, two of whom were based in New York to look after American sales.

To conclude this brief summary of Ewart's first century, by 1889 it was employing between 5000 and 6000 workers, with an annual wages bill of £150,000. It operated 33,500 spindles and 2000 power looms.

Linen and Belfast

The linen industry has long been regarded as crucial to the development of Belfast. Curiously, however, in the first flush of industrialisation, cotton was king. Linen had long been produced as a cottage industry, but it was to be many decades before it could be manufactured on an industrial scale. This was in large part owing to the difficulty of spinning flax mechanically: the fibres are brittle and break easily, so continued to be hand spun until the introduction from around 1826 of the wet spinning process, in which a humid atmosphere made the fibre more suitable for machine spinning. Hence the late move (1840) into flax spinning by Ewart's.

Similarly, the weaving of linen had remained largely a rural cottage industry, with brown linen being produced by individual weavers and then sold to merchants for bleaching and finishing. The invention of wet spinning made it possible to transfer resources from cotton, where the competition from the huge and more cost-effective English and Scottish manufacturers was squeezing out their Irish counterparts, to linen, where Ulster already had a strong lead. By 1853 a Captain Gilbert was able to write:

> The great staple of manufacture in Belfast and its vicinity is linen, and the spinning and weaving of linen yarn. From a recent trade report of this district I find that in the year 1829 there was only one mill, containing 15,000 spindles. In 1850 the number had increased to 326,000, and at the commencement of the present year they had reached 500,000 spindles, upwards of 100,000 having been added in 1852.[4]

An important contribution of the industry to Belfast's prosperity was the employment it gave to large numbers of females. This made the city attractive to skilled male workers in other industries, notably shipbuilding, since it meant that the combined incomes of women and men enabled a much higher standard of living in the average household than was possible in other British towns which relied exclusively on heavy industry. In fact, nearly half the manufacturing workers in Belfast in 1905 were female, a remarkably high proportion in an industrial city.

It is also worth noting that linen, although seen for many years as the leading industry of 'Protestant' Ulster, employed large numbers of Catholics in its workforce, 70 per cent of which consisted of women. One observer, who worked in the textile industry for many years from 1903, stated that the female workers in the mills were predominantly Catholic, while about three-quarters of weavers were Protestant, but that they worked together harmoniously.[5]

My own experience of the industry was limited to visits to the mill and factory in the 1950s, guided by my grandfather Victor. The lasting impressions these left on me were: the evocative smell of the raw flax piled up in bins; the bewildering sight of thousands of spindles in motion; the skill of workers rapidly repairing broken threads; the ear-shattering noise of the looms; and the almost magical process of damask weaving, from the cards fed into the looms to the shimmering cloth emerging from the machines. But the most enduring memory is of the women workers paddling about barefoot in the mill rooms – 'wet spinning' – one of whom Victor proudly singled out as the recently elected 'Irish Linen Queen' for that year. There was much discussion from the mid-19th century onwards of the harmful, or (some argued) beneficial, effects of these working conditions, but I can witness that nothing had really changed. The temperature was about 32 degrees C. and the atmosphere very humid, with quantities of water spraying off the wet fibres. It may well be that the employers provided waterproof clothing, but that workers would not wear it because of the heat and perspiration engendered by the process.

In those days, it was a common experience when travelling through the Ulster countryside to encounter the strong but not unpleasant smell of flax 'retting' in the streams and ponds. The purpose of retting was to soften the outer husks of the flax to render them easier to comb out or 'scutch' from the inner fibres, in preparation for spinning. It is wonderfully described in the opening lines of Seamus Heaney's poem 'Death of a Naturalist':

All year the flax-dam festered in the heart
Of the townland; green and heavy headed
Flax had rotted there, weighted down by huge sods.
Daily it sweltered in the punishing sun.
Bubbles gargled delicately, bluebottles
Wove a strong gauze of sound around the smell.[6]

Sir William Ewart and his connections

At one time there were three generations of William Ewarts working as partners in the firm, William Ewart III joining his father and grandfather in 1843. His considerable wealth and position as one of Belfast's major industrialists enabled him to take a leading role in municipal affairs.

As we have seen from the inscription on our silver salver, he served as Mayor in 1859 and 1860. In 1878 he won a by-election and became MP for Belfast City, as a Conservative. He held the seat in 1880 and occupied it until 1885, when the new seat of Belfast North was created, winning it in turn and holding it until his death in 1889. In the family archives there are several letters from him on the headed notepaper of his London residence, his political commitments obliging him to spend considerable periods each year in the capital while Parliament was in session. His successor in the seat was Sir Edward Harland, joint founder of Harland and Wolff, the shipbuilders whose mighty crane has been preserved and dominates the tourist area now known as the 'Titanic Quarter' in Belfast.

Ewart was President of the Irish Linen Trade and Flax Supply Associations, a member of the Belfast Local Marine Board, and a magistrate for Antrim and Belfast. On 13 September 1887 his outstanding record of public service was rewarded with the Baronetcy 'of Glenmachan in Strandtown in the County of Down and of Glenbank in Belfast in the County of Antrim'.

In light of later developments within the family, it is significant that Sir William was a strong supporter of the Church of Ireland, like the Scottish Episcopalians a sister church within the Anglican communion (two of his sons, Richard Hooker and George Herbert, were named after prominent early Anglican divines). His involvement with church matters is well summarised by Richard Froggatt[7]:

> Ewart was chairman of a group of trustees who acquired a site (known as 'Bunker Hill') just east of Belfast (though today well within the built-up area) for the building of a

Sir William Ewart

parish church. Unusually, no local architect was chosen, the trustees preferring to commission the celebrated English church architect William Butterfield. The original plans were not fulfilled until 1891, when William Ewart's family provided the necessary funds as a memorial to him. The church, St Mark's, Dundela, has two windows dedicated to members of William Ewart's family: to his widow, Isabella Kelso Mathewson, and to his son, the 2nd baronet, Sir William Quartus Ewart. The church is well-known worldwide as the parish church of C.S.Lewis, the internationally-acclaimed academic and religious polemicist, who was himself a relative of the Ewart family (his mother was a cousin of Mary Warren Heard, who was married to Sir William Quartus Ewart; Lewis describes his close ties to the family in his autobiography). William Ewart was a member of the Representative Body of the (now named) Church of Ireland, set up under the Irish Church Act 1869, after the disestablishment of the Church; this body was created to hold and administer Church property. (It is mere coincidence that the Prime Minister who implemented

> this development was named William Ewart Gladstone.) *The Northern Whig* newspaper paid tribute to Ewart's successful exertions on behalf of his Church when it obituarised that 'there was hardly a church throughout Belfast which had not received of his liberality'. He died in London, at 14 Albemarle Street, Piccadilly, and was buried in Belfast five days later. The *Northern Whig* had referred to him as 'father of our staple trade in Belfast'.

St Mark's, Dundela is indeed a remarkable church, a fine example of the work of William Butterfield (architect of Keble College, Oxford and All Saints' Margaret Street, London), in his signature style of polychrome brickwork. It is now a place of pilgrimage for C.S.Lewis fans from all over the world.

The description of the Ewart family in Lewis's autobiography *Surprised by Joy* is worth quoting in full, both for its affectionate recall of Belfast upper-middle class life at the time, and for the budding writer's romantic view of his glamorous cousins:

> Less than a mile from our home stood the largest house I then knew, which I will here call Mountbracken [Glenmachan] and there lived Sir W. E. [William Quartus Ewart, 2nd Baronet but fourth William Ewart]. Lady E. was my mother's first cousin and perhaps my mother's dearest friend, and it was no doubt for my mother's sake that she took upon herself the heroic work of civilising my brother and me.
>
> We had a standing invitation to lunch at Mountbracken whenever we were at home; to this, almost entirely, we owe it that we did not grow up savages. The debt is not only to Lady E. ('Cousin Mary') but to her whole family; walks, motor-drives (in those days an exciting novelty), picnics, and invitations to the theatre were showered on us, year after year, with a kindness which our rawness, our noise, and our unpunctuality never seemed to weary.
>
> We were at home there almost as much as in our own house, but with this great difference, that a certain standard of manners had to be kept up. Whatever I know (it is not much) of courtesy and savoir faire I learned at Mountbracken.
>
> Sir W. ('Cousin Quartus') was the eldest of several brothers who owned between them one of the most important industrial concerns in Belfast. He belonged

in fact to just that class and generation of which the modern man gets his impressions through Galsworthy's Forsytes. Unless Cousin Quartus was very untrue to type (as he may well have been) that impression is grossly unjust. No one less like a Galsworthian character ever existed. He was gracious, childlike, deeply and religiously humble, and abounding in charity. No man could feel more fully his responsibility to dependants. He had a good deal of boyish gaiety about him; at the same time I always felt that the conception of duty dominated his life. His stately figure, his grey beard, and his strikingly handsome profile make up one of the most venerable images in my memory.

Physical beauty was indeed common to most of the family. Cousin Mary was the very type of the beautiful old lady, with her silver hair and her sweet Southern Irish voice; foreigners must be warned that this resembles what they call a 'brogue' about as little as the speech of a Highland gentleman resembles the jargon of the Glasgow slums.

Mary Warren (Heard) Ewart ("Cousin Mary')

But it was the three daughters whom we knew best. All three were 'grown up' but in fact much nearer to us in age than any other grown-ups we knew, and all three were strikingly handsome. H. [Charlotte Hope], the eldest and the gravest, was a Juno, a dark queen who at certain moments looked like a Jewess. K. [Isabella Kelso] was more like a Valkyrie (though all, I think, were good horse-women) with her father's profile. There was in her face something of the delicate fierceness of a thoroughbred horse, an indignant fineness of nostril, the possibility of an excellent disdain. She had what the vanity of my own sex calls a 'masculine' honesty; no man ever was a truer friend. As for the youngest, G. [Mary Gundreda], I can only say that she was the most beautiful woman I have ever seen, perfect in shape and colour and voice and every movement – but who can describe beauty?

The reader may smile at this as the far-off echo of a precocious calf-love, but he will be wrong. There are

> beauties so unambiguous that they need no lens of that kind to reveal them; they are visible even to the careless and objective eyes of a child.
>
> In some ways Mountbracken was like our Father's house. There too we found the attics, the indoor silences, the endless bookshelves. In the early days, when we were still only a quarter tamed, we often neglected our hostesses and rummaged on our own; it was there that I found Lubbock's *Ants, Bees and Wasps*. But it was also very different. Life there was more spacious and considered than with us, glided like a barge where ours bumped like a cart.[8]

Later in the book Lewis remarks that, while he did not feel it appropriate to enter into an exhaustive account of his small circle of family and friends in Belfast, he has had to speak of the household at Glenmachan 'because the story of my life could not be told without it'. In tracing the overwhelming importance of 'Northernness' in his intellectual development – Icelandic sagas, Wagner, William Morris – he recalls how, soon after he had become fascinated with this world, he went to stay for several weeks with the eldest Ewart daughter, now married, in Dundrum, near Dublin.

> There, on the drawing-room table, I found the very book which had started the whole affair and which I had never dared to hope I should see, *Siegfried and the Twilight of the Gods*, illustrated by Arthur Rackham.[9]

I visited Glenmachan House only once, I think, with my cousin Philippa, and explored the grounds and greenhouse with her. I have a vague impression of 'Cousin Gundred', a stately old lady; and of her daughter Primrose, another striking horsewoman. Philippa and my other Belfast cousins will remember her much better.

Clive Staples Lewis was the second son of a solicitor living at a house called 'Little Lea' in Strandtown, a prosperous suburb on the eastern outskirts of Belfast. In my first year of reading English at Cambridge (1962-3) I 'sat at the feet' of Lewis, known as 'Jack' to his friends and fellow-dons. He had moved there in 1954 from Oxford to take up the Chair of Medieval and Renaissance Literature, and lectured to us on medieval poetry. By this time he had achieved worldwide fame, not so much for his scholarly writings, but for his many works of popular Christian apologetics and the phenomenally successful *Narnia* books for children. In the USA he enjoyed almost cult status, and my abiding memory is of an American girl sitting next to me spending the whole lecture drawing Lewis as a sort of demi-god on a dais, surrounded by adoring worshippers. Unfortunately I recall almost nothing of the content of the lectures except a lengthy analysis of Lagamon's *Brut*, an obscure Middle English poem which, to my shame, I never got round to reading (several minutes were spent debating whether the poet's name should be pronounced 'Layamon' or 'Lagamon'). We were not to know then that Lewis was so near the end of his life. He died on 22 November 1963, a week before his 65th birthday – the very day and, by a sad coincidence, within an hour, of the assassination of President John F. Kennedy.

The name 'Gundreda' is so unusual that it calls for a note of explanation. Gundred Ewart's mother, Mary Warren Heard, claimed kinship with the ancient family of De Warenne. A woman named 'Gundred' or 'Gundreda' was the Flemish-born wife of William de Warenne, who fought with William the Conqueror at the Battle of Hastings and was granted the earldom of Surrey in 1088. It has often been claimed that she was a bastard daughter of William the Conqueror, but this is disputed. She and her husband established Lewes Priory in Sussex.

The preoccupation with claiming 'Norman blood' in one's family line was widespread through the 19th century, and reflects the aspirations to gentility of the prosperous business and professional classes. As we shall see, Thomas William Clarendon spent considerable time and effort trying to establish descent from the Black Prince, and there is plenty of evidence of the fashion in fiction of the time. By the end of the century, enthusiasm for it was beginning to fade: in *Tess of the D'Urbervilles* (1891), Thomas Hardy was able to satirise the whole culture of false gentility. The seeds of Tess Durbeyfield's tragedy are sown when a local parson of antiquarian leanings tells her father that his poverty-stricken peasant family are the only remaining descendants of the noble line of the D'Urbervilles. This unsettling information leads directly to her being encouraged by her parents to pay court to the wealthy D'Urberville family, who, by a nice irony, have no ancestral connection to the name at all but have merely taken it off the shelf to enhance their image. Hence follow her seduction by Alec D'Urberville, ruin and death. By a further irony, Tess's family *are* in the true line of descent, but much good does it do them: it is money that rules, while an ancient name is at best irrelevant, at worst a curse.

Enter the Clarendons

'Cousin Quartus' was one of 14 children of Sir William the 1st baronet, not all of whom survived infancy. His younger sister Lavinia, born in 1853, was to become the crucial link between the Ewart and Clarendon families when, on 22 April 1879, she married the Rev. Thomas William Clarendon.

The Clarendons are an old-established Anglo-Irish family who may have first arrived in Ireland in the early 17th century, in the shape of a soldier, Cornet Clarendon, who was awarded some land, possibly in Co. Meath. The crest of its coat-of-arms (or 'achievement' in the language of heraldry) consists of a Prince of Wales feather with bars across it, which has led to speculation that the family could have been descended from an illegitimate son of Edward the Black Prince (1330-76). There is correspondence in the archive between Rev. Thomas William and the College of Arms in Dublin, undertaken in an attempt to have this claim officially validated, but to no avail. Above is the whole achievement as it appears on a bookplate.

We are on firmer ground if we start with Thomas William's father, Frederick Villiers Clarendon (1820-1904), whose career is well documented[10]. The aspirations of the family to gentility are clearly signalled by the decision to use the names 'Frederick Villiers', frequently borne by sons of the Earls of Clarendon. His father was a linen draper and estate owner of Westmoreland Street in Dublin. He was born in 1820 and entered Trinity College at the age of 14, graduating BA in 1839. He worked for the whole of his career as a civil engineer and architect for the Board of Works, from 1854 as Surveyor of Works and Buildings, until his retirement in 1887. His early work was concerned with the design of prisons and asylums, but his best-known building is the Irish Natural History Museum in Merrion Street, now part of the National Museum of Ireland. He provided his services free of charge to design the Mariners' Hall in Howth in 1867, which then served as a Presbyterian Meeting House for over thirty years: its services were conducted in Scottish Gaelic, the language of the immigrant seasonal fishermen of the village. He died at his home in Mountjoy Square in 1904.

The connection with the Clarendons began with the marriage in 1873 of his daughter Mary Elizabeth ('Maimée') to Lavinia Ewart's elder brother Lavens Mathewson Ewart of Glenbank, Belfast. Mary was just one year older than her brother Thomas William (1855-1934), so it was probably through his sister that he was introduced to the Ewart family and was to meet his future bride. The relationships become clear when one reads the following charming 'thank you' letter, written after Christmas 1890, from the rectory at Maralin. By this time Lavinia had her own children: Dorothy, Randal, and Victor.

Lavinia Clarendon (née Ewart) to her mother-in-law Margàret Clarendon (née Slacke)

Maralin
Dec 27.90

My dear Mother
I have so much to thank you for that I don't know where to begin – First, for the own particular book, which is lovely & for the delightful box of biscuits – & indeed for all the contents of the big hamper – which gave great pleasure in the disclosing thereof, but I could not help thinking how tired the fingers must be that tied up all the many parcels. I enclose Randal's note . D. [Dorothy] has written to my mother today, & in time will write to you. As Victor [aged 3] cannot yet express himself by letter I must send his thanks for the dear little stable &

the sweets, & I think everything gave great pleasure. We had grand fun opening everything – & indeed it was thank God a very happy Xmas & I trust also with you.

I hope to write to the girls Father and Owen as soon as I can – I am sure Lavens & Maime had a happy Xmas together.

We had a lovely day yesterday, seeing all our friends – there were 54 at the party not the least welcome being Herbert and Alice & Ernest & Clement. The Burkes came, even Mrs! The tree was very pretty & there was a gift for each – Mrs Johnston & I made many of them, which was wise in these hard times.

Dorothy wore a pale blue smocked dress which Fred sent her, & she looked quite pretty. Mrs Johnston does her hair very becomingly on these occasions. Randal was happy as a king, especially in having the Glenbank boys – & when I was putting him to bed he said 'it was lovely to see the younger children enjoying themselves' – Dear little Victor has had a grand Christmas. We had the Greers on Xmas Day – & dining at 5.30 after Carol Service – to which he came down, & he had a splendid time – Next morning when I met him I said 'How are you after Christmas Day' – He replied emphatically 'Jolly!'

Father Christmas presented him with a hamper of sweets – & presently Mrs Johnston noticed him going alone out of the dining room where the tree was going on, & she followed him – She found him in the nursery by himself 'I just came up to lave some of my sweets for Nan [his nanny?]. I'm seeing which she wd like best' – and there he had a little pile on the table for her – Wasn't it sweet of him?

Mrs Johnston has gone today to Major Bromfield in Belfast to stay till Tuesday. She has been a great help in many ways. Ernest told Mary she (Mrs. J.) was the only lady here worth looking at!

We have had a nice resting day, & tidying up day too – both of which were needed after the dissipations.

Fond love to all
Ever yr loving child
Vinnie

But this is to anticipate. In 1879 Thomas William (henceforth TW) was a impecunious young student, in training for the ministry at 'College' in Belfast. He had already obtained an MA and BD from Trinity College, Dublin, where he collected a number of academic prizes. Now about to finish his training, he is seeking his first job, and is anxious to be married and set up home as soon as possible. His future father-in-law, Sir William Ewart, MP, who is about to depart for London and his Parliamentary duties, naturally counsels prudence. He tries to advise the young couple for the best in the important dilemma they face: furnished or unfurnished? The following letter, though lengthy, is quoted in full, both for the light it throws on the three personalities involved and for its richness in period detail. It is especially illuminating in its reflections of class attitudes and of what was fitting for a curate at the start of his career, with little money available but an obligation to keep up certain standards. Poor Lavinia, having to contemplate living in a 'row' (terrace)! TW's numbered arguments for and against, perhaps unsurprisingly given the subject of his studies, read like a gentle parody of an exercise in theological debate.

Rev. Thomas William Clarendon to Lavinia Ewart

> 4 Fountainville Avenue
> Feb.3, 1879.
>
> My own darling. It was awfully hard for me to have to go away when I wanted so badly to stay & comfort you but I am very glad to find you became peaceful & happy so soon. You are not to take this morning as an allegory of our lives – I promise not to be always calmly discussing the parallelism of Hebrew poetry when you are worried with domestic cares. I shall claim my fair share in them & I think we shall find them lighter by bearing them together.
>
> I am afraid you will be disappointed to find that I have very little to tell. I had only a few minutes talk with your Father – in the office and in the carriage between Bedford St. & the College.
>
> He said we must take time to consider the matter, that he had only heard of it after he had put on his coat to leave home this morning, that he thought it was better for us to take a furnished house, & that he had heard of one in Univ. Sq., that I might be only a short time in Belfast, 'Lavinia doesn't like the idea of living in a row but she could get over that.'

If we were to live in a villa like that of Mrs. Workman's we should require a carriage. That he had never heard of a curate furnishing a house. &c.

All very kindly said. I answered that it was the fact of his having to go away so soon that had brought the subject up so quickly – that I thought I should probably be at least five years at Saint Thomas's for that I did not know any other place where I could get such good training or any other man that I should prefer to be with, that there could accordingly be no reason for taking any other curacy & I was quite certain I should not get an incumbency sooner – even if I were offered one I should not think it my duty except under very peculiar circumstances to take the sole charge of a parish when so young & untrained. He still said he was sure I would not be five years at S. Thomas' though he thought I could not be in a better place as curate.

I said there would not be the slightest necessity for our having a carriage if we were to live in 'Eden' – that I thought hiring furniture a very unsatisfactory thing – that we should not require much to begin with but that on the whole it was an important subject and required consideration. He did not give me much opportunity for speaking & the whole conversation took a few minutes.

Afterwards in the carriage I asked him had he been thinking of any particular time for the wedding. I told him that we had been thinking & talking in an informal way of April 22nd. It would be the first day of the synod, he would be back from London &c. He asked me when would Easter be. I said the 13th and he then said 'Well yes that would be a very convenient time unless we should say April 1880 or December 1879.' I said I could not do without my wife all that time, that it would be very different if he had not to be in London the greater part of the year & that I wanted to get properly to work at the Parish. He 'I think we ought to postpone all this sort of thing until you are out of College.' T. 'Oh I am out of College now to all intents and purposes & should have quite done with it in March, besides you are going away so soon that I think we ought to see something about it before you go.' 'Yes there's something in that but we must take time to consider it.'

I stayed at the College for the ceremony. I was very much interested in Lord Dufferin's speech but I thought we were going to look at the house after it – but no! Your Father drove to town with Sir Thomas Maclure & I came home. Jack Preston got your father to introduce his to me & congratulated me very warmly saying I was the most fortunate man in the world. I said I felt very happy & he said I had good reason. So, darling, I think he is a very wise young man , with particularly nice teeth.

I quite feel with you about the furnished house business, ma mie, but don't you see that it would hardly be good taste for me to say much about it? And I think you were right not to vex your Father by persistence, all the same if you could find a good opportunity for talking the whole matter over calmly with him 'under four eyes' or if Helen could do it I think these are our strong points.

1. The difference between the rent of a furnished house & that of a smaller unfurnished house would probably in five years come to more or as much , or at any rate very little less than the cost of furnishing now, & in the former case we should have nothing to show for all that money when going into our rectory & should have to spend exactly the same amount then as we should have to spend now. Whereas in the latter case we should have our own furniture. (When I was a child my father used to take us out to Clontarf [to the north of Dublin, by the sea] frequently but sometimes I used to get a penny trunk [whistle?] to console me for staying at home when Maimée went. I remember I used to think the trunk is something that lasts whereas the drive is all over in a short time. It's very much the same.) Accordingly I should like to borrow money from my father (I know he would do it) for furnishing now and pay back by degrees.
2. It is not as if I were in the army & we might be moved off to the Cape and have to sell our furniture for whatever we could get for it, but any incumbency I would get would probably be either in this Diocese or the Diocese of Dublin & we should not have to move more than 100 miles so we could easily (& we with our heart-strings twined round it would most <u>certainly</u>) bring our own furniture with us.
3. Your argument. We could not get a furnished house for long in Belfast.
4. An aesthetic argument. The furniture of almost any

moderately-sized house in Belfast would most probably have some part of it vulgar or in bad taste – & ma mie that would be a daily worry perhaps for years.

5. We can get a house with decent-sized living rooms of which we need only furnish some rooms, by paying a little more, but if we get a furnished house with decent-sized living rooms we shall have a whole lot of furnished rooms which we shall not want but for the furniture of which we shall have to pay e.g. Let x be the price of the price of an unfurnished house & $x+\gamma$ the price of the same house furnished & $x-\alpha$ = the price of the used part of the house then α will = what we should waste, whereas in the case of the furnished house we should waste $\alpha + \alpha/\gamma$ Take x = £50 γ = £30 α = £10. Then we should lose £10 in one case & £13 in the other. I am afraid I have not made the thing clearer by algebra.
6. It would not be home-like and it would hardly be respectable to go into the rectory with a lot of spick & span new furniture, after being married for five years.
7. If our friends thought we were furnishing now they would give us things for the house instead of personal things as wedding presents & so we should not have so many things to buy as we should have 5 years hence.
8. The strongest of all to us. We want to have associations of our early married life.
9. Argument from authority. All young married people of my acquaintance have either furnished at once or else have regretted that they did not do so.

Against all these arguments there is

1. We should be better able to furnish when I am a rector, but that could easily be got over by borrowing money as I said before.
2. It would give us time to look about us. But I have always thought that the most uncomfortable sort of life to lead. People ought to settle down when they marry. Besides we should be spending money unprofitably the while.
3. A house we would furnish ourselves would be plainer than one we would hire. – But the things would be our very own.
4. Your father never heard of a curate furnishing. That is because there are so few married curates, but J.B.Crozier furnished.

I think this is a tolerably complete examination of the matter but it has taken so much time that I can only write a little more.

I worked satisfactorily to-day on the whole.

I am delighted to hear it will be Wednesday & not later that we shall meet & I think we shall be very happy, darling, don't you?

My pen & paper & writing are wretchedly bad to-night, and I have several times written wrong words. I must be in love. With whom?

Mr Hamilton knows exactly & Dr. Chadwick is right as far as he goes. I like the idea of Anna McKinley [?] very much but would Marian come as cook?

I shall write my sermon all if I have time.

If there should be any change in your arrangements for Wednesday please let me know.

If your father would like to go to see any houses, furnished or unfurnished, with me, he will find me here at any hour.

My very own darling you are quite right. God has given us so much happiness that it would be very ungrateful of us to be cast down because we cannot arrange our affairs as we would wish.

Good night God bless you my very own

Ever your loving
T. William Clarendon

Standing: Lavinia and her sister-in-law Margaret Clarendon. Seated: (left) Mary 'Maimée' (Clarendon) Ewart; (right) Helen Ewart

TW and Lavinia in later life

There are further letters extant from TW, some discussing with Sir William the terms of the marriage settlement, others pondering his vocation and where to take up his first curacy. In 1878 he was ordained curate at St Thomas's. A few years later he was offered the choice of two livings, and chose the poorer, rural parish of Magheralin in Co. Down, where he felt he could do more useful work, becoming Rector in 1884. (The name was always shortened by the family – or anglicised? – to 'Maralin'.) There was an existing family connection to Maralin: his mother was the daughter of the Rev. William Randal Slacke, who had been curate there. In 1908 TW and Lavinia erected two stained glass windows in the church as memorials to their respective parents.[11]

There is an interesting exchange of letters between TW and Lavinia on the subject of images, a potent source of controversy ranging Roman Catholics and High Anglicans on one side of the argument, and Low Church and Dissenting congregations on the other. The correspondence acknowledges the power and beauty of the best images to inspire faith, but in the Ulster context this was a dangerous issue. Indeed, it caused serious trouble later on in the parish when TW, as rector, was accused of Popish tendencies in the measures he took to beautify the church. This distressing episode occurred at the time of its consecration in 1891, after it had been rebuilt under his direction. For a full account of the controversy, which centred on the installation of a new reredos with 'crocketed finials', mistakenly viewed by the extreme Protestant element in the congregation as 'crosses', see the parish history, *Like an Evening Gone.*[12] However, his career blossomed, and he became in due time 'Rector of Maralin and Dean of the Diocese of Dromore'. He was able to afford trips to Italy to look at art and churches, as evidenced by an 1893 edition of Baedeker's *Central Italy and Rome* bearing his signature and bookplate. One is reminded of E.M. Forster's portrayal of clergymen touring Italy, Baedeker in hand, in *A Room with a View.* Could Forster have met TW? It's an intriguing thought.

Lavinia died in 1913. A touching relic which remains is a lock of her fine, auburn hair, a characteristic inherited by many of her descendants. TW survived her, through the grim years of war and depression, until 1934. In a biographical sketch of 'Dean Clarendon', it was noted that 'When employment was scarce he secured jobs for many of the men folk in the village at Ewart's Linen Factory in Belfast'.[13]

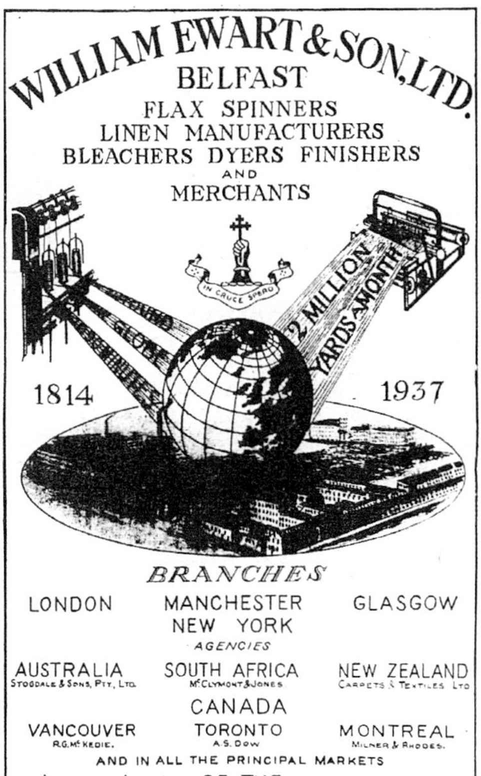

Depression-proof? A 1937 Ewart's advertisement

2 American Interlude: The Jones Family in Ireland and the USA

'Dear little Victor' Clarendon grew up to marry Nina Virginia Gregory Jones, an American, in 1911. This bare statement records another momentous conjunction of two families in our story. As it happens, Nina's roots were also firmly in Ireland, on her father's side, but on her mother's the American generations go back much further. Let us begin with the former.

Family life and the professions in 19th century Ireland

Isaac Jones, who had owned and run a school at Gorey, Co. Wexford, was forced out of his house and lands by civil unrest during the United Irishmen rebellion of 1798. He moved to Rathfarnham, south of Dublin, and in 1802, with his son Thomas, set up Nutgrove School, an academy for young gentlemen. A very early newspaper prospectus of 14 July 1807, later framed together with silhouettes of Thomas and Isaac, sets out the school's terms.

The annual fee or 'Salary' of thirty guineas covered 'Board,

Nutgrove School prospectus 1807

and Education for the *University*, the *Army*, the *Navy*, or *Business*.' Unlike Dotheboys Hall in *Nicholas Nickleby*, where the main attraction for parents anxious to dump their offspring was Mr Squeers's promise of 'No vacations!', the Nutgrove boys enjoyed two holidays a year: a month in summer and a week in winter. '*Washing and mending Clothes*' and, '*Wine*, a Glass daily', were each charged at one guinea a quarter. French and Dancing were also available as extras.

The school prospered, attracting the sons of members of the army, church and professions, and of well-to-do businessmen. It was held in high regard, as evidenced by the roll call of the great and good who attended the funeral of Philip Jones in 1861 (Philip had taken over the running of the school on his father Thomas's death).

Mary Gregory Jones; Philip Jones

The newspaper report of this occasion, to be found in the 'red album' described later, expressed satisfaction that the school would be continued by Mrs Jones, whose 'remarkable attention paid ... to the domestic comfort of the boys is appreciated by all who know the school'. As an amusing instance of these domestic arrangements, my cousin Eily Watson, her grand-daughter, recalled her saying that she was 'asked by parents who's boys wore flannel shirts to see the shirt was changed every 2 weeks and hung up to air, but never washed!'[14] Eily also sent me a remarkable photograph of Philip and the boys at the school, taken in around 1855. He is in the centre of the back row, wearing a wide-brimmed hat. The informality of the poses, the variety of dress and headgear, and the casually held cricket bats, suggest a benign institution where individuality was allowed to flourish.

Some indication of the cultivated gentility of the Nutgrove

Philip Jones and pupils, Nutgrove School c.1855

household and its milieu is contained in two albums which survive, one red, one black. They contain many pencil sketches, probably by Philip, of conventional landscape and figure subjects in the style of Turner, the Dutch, and other masters, some of them copies, others taken directly from the subject; also views cut out and pasted in from printed sources; and poems in manuscript by several hands.

The manuscript poems include, in the 'red album': 'Remembrance' by TFAG, 21 March 1846; a mourning poem to a dead boy, by E. Jones with a silhouette of its subject; 'To Nannie, on feeling that she has changed' by WAK, Sep, 9.1842; 'A Charade' (shades of Jane Austen!) , 'A Valentine' by WAK, Feb.14.1840; 'Lines written on visiting Nutgrove three years after being at School there' by John Garnett; and a *decoupage* wreath of delicately cut flowers pasted onto a sheet of paper, with accompanying verse, by A.J. 21 July 1863. On one page are mounted cuttings of the reports of Philip's funeral, referred to above.

The 'black album' bears Philip Jones's bookplate on its inside front cover. There is no record of any full coat-of-arms for the Jones family, so the boar's head may simply have been adopted as a form of identification. If my memory serves correctly, my mother possessed a signet ring with the device, which could have been used for sealing documents. Unfortunately it was stolen in a burglary when she was living in sheltered housing near the end of her life, in the 1990s.

The contents of this album are similar but more sparse, with, in manuscript, another 'Charade' and, more significantly, 'Lines addressed to the Memory of my Father': these are written out in beautiful copperplate and headed by the same silhouette of Thomas Jones as accompanies the 1807 prospectus. They seek to establish Thomas's claim to public remembrance on the same grounds as are set out in an undated newspaper cutting of the mid-19th century, supplied by Cousin Eily with the 1855 school photograph. The cutting is more detailed and explicit. In a paragraph of tribute to 'Tom' (re-christened 'Jerry' by his pupils!), the writer remembers that

> Long before the date of Mr Anthony Blake's commission, or of Mr Stanley's National Board, Mr Jones published proposals of an eminently practical character for a system of general education in Ireland, as the best foundation for its internal peace and advancement. The establishment of a permanent constabulary force – decidedly the best Irish Institution of the present century – was first recommended by him; and with that establishment he proposed to connect another, less acceptable at the time, but of which the value is now scarcely disputed – we mean that of a stipendiary magistracy, dependent on the government and responsible to it, for providing against the possible 'perversion of justice in a province'.

Tom Jones lived to see most of these far- sighted ideas adopted, the piece concludes, only for others to take the credit, 'to the great glorification of their supposed authors'.

The most poignant treasure to be found in the albums is a small collection, loosely inserted, of letters and drawings by the talented 'J.J.' I have not been able to discover his identity, but the illustrated letter reproduced and transcribed here is written on 'Strandtown, Belfast' headed notepaper, and he was clearly a friend or relative of the family at Nutgrove. Strandtown was not a house but a suburb of Belfast (where C.S. Lewis grew up, as noted above). 'Jack' may have actually *lived* at 'Lisderry', or 'Lisenderry', Co. Tyrone (see below).The letter talks of 'Waller' and 'Mary', both daughters of Philip Jones (and later to be aunts of Nina), but is addressed to 'Violet', whom I have so far been unable to trace. She could have been the third daughter, Emily, and 'Violet' could have been a nickname or a second forename.

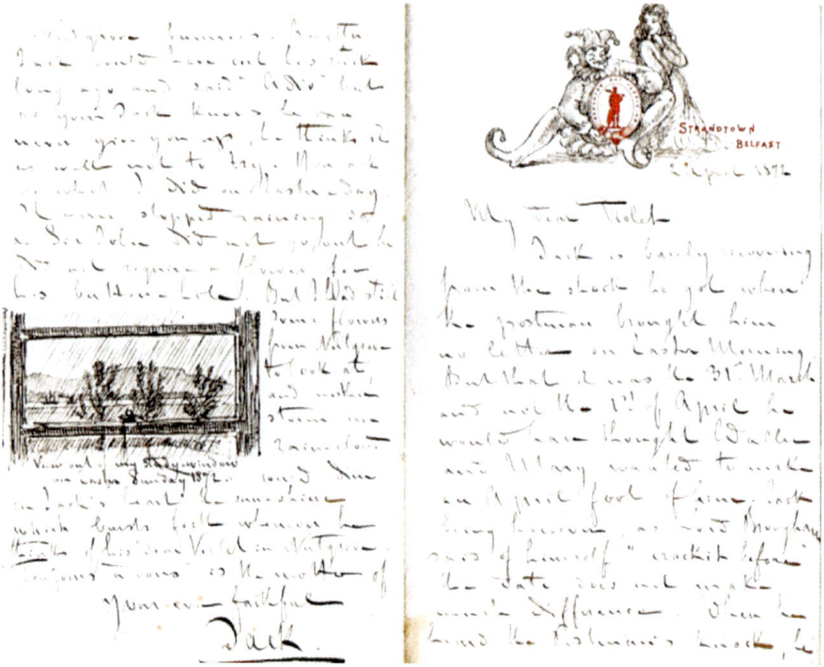

Pages 1 (right) and 4 (left), the opening and closing pages.

It is a teasing and affectionate *jeu d'esprit* penned for the amusement of its young recipients. One can only speculate as to who the rival, 'Louis D.', could be!

The complete letter, dated 2 April 1872, transcribes as:

> [printed roundel of a wild man with club and shield, and motto 'deficiam aut perficiam', meaning 'I will perish or succeed', surrounded by a drawing of 'Jack' the writer as a jester, and the girl, Violet.]

> My dear Violet
>
> Jack is barely recovering from the shock he got when the postman brought him no letter on Easter Morning. But that it was the 31st of March and not the 1st of April he would have thought Waller and Mary wanted to make an April fool of him. Jack being however, as Lord Brougham

said of himself "crackit before" the date does not make much difference. When he heard the Postman's Knock, he

[p.2]

made a rush to the Hall-door but when instead of letters from his Pets he was only handed a shabby newspaper he was thrown on his back and felt as if he never would get up.

You must know that Jack wore the slippers for the first time on Easter Sunday, as his domestic "Ogre" would not let him put them on before, but when he

[p.3]

has them on he really looks as if somebody cared about him. Whilst he was wondering why his pets did not write to him a horrible idea struck him, namely that at the commencement of the holidays he had been thrown into a corner together with lapons[?], schoolbooks and other hateful things. But since this morning he is all right again, as "wild" as a March hare and as merry as a cricket, singing and whistling all day long, all because he knows he is not quite forgotten. Though what with the ? ? running away with my capital (girl) and what with this news of another robber prying on my preserves whose name is Louis D. & who evidently wants my Moll I have many a round to bring against my

[p.4]

Nutgrove bunnies. Another Jack would have had out his stick long ago and said "Go To" but as your Jack knows he can never give you up, he thinks as well not to try. You ask me what I did on Easter Day. It never stopped raining so as Sir John did not go out he did not require a flower for his buttonhole. But I had still

View out of my study-window on Easter Sunday 1872

some flowers from Nutgrove to look at, and within storm nor rain-cloud could dim in Jack's heart the sun-shine which bursts forth whenever he thinks of his dear Violet in Nutgrove. "Toujours á vous" is the motto of

Your ever faithful

Jack

As a pendant to this letter, here is Jack's rendering of a bunny postman, drawn on the lid of a cardboard box.

The remaining two items in this group are 'A new Ballad/ most humbly dedicated/ to/ Lady W...r/ by Sir J..n/ Lisderry July 1871', in similar style to the letter, and 'Ye stolen Violet!' a poem beneath a coloured drawing of a weeping Cupid and two lovers,

with Nutgrove in the background, surrounded by a decorative border of violet leaves, flowers and tendrils, which incorporates the words 'An mein liebes Veilchen' ('To my dear Violet') in German Gothic script.

The ballad manuscript includes a drawing of the Lisderry and Nutgrove houses. I have no information at present on 'Lisderry', but the drawing closely corresponds to a printed engraving of 'Lisenderry, Co. Tyrone' in the black album. (It may be that Lisenderry Golf Club, on the outskirts of Aughnacloy, now occupies the site of this house.)

Nina's third forename is Gregory, commemorating Irish forebears on her grandmother's side. The most significant material link to this family is a large oil portrait of Mrs Anne Gregory, her great-great grandmother, at present gracing our hall. Born Anne Van Treight, her father was Dr George Van Treight of Leightin Bridge near Carlow, who is named in an 1804 muster-roll of the Kilkenny Legion[15], a volunteer corps made up of local gentry and traders. It is noteworthy, given the later polarisation of Irish society, that at least half of them were Roman Catholics. These informal militia bodies were assembled at times of perceived danger from foreign wars or civil unrest: it should be remembered that the major rebellion by the United Irishmen had occurred as recently as 1798.

Anne married Dr William Gregory, who ran Finglass (modern spelling 'Finglas') Private Mental Home in Dublin. Her eldest son, Richard Reed Gregory (uncle of Nina's grandmother, Mary

Portrait of Anne (Van Treight) Gregory

Gregory, who married Philip Jones of Nutgrove), succeeded his father at Finglass. He was a Member of the Royal College of Surgeons in Ireland and the first Master of the Coombe Lying-In Hospital (originally located on a site known as Dean Swift's Vineyard, Heytesbury Street, Dublin) from 1829-31. The following passage, while in some respects casting rather a negative light on the Finglass institution, provides a fascinating insight into the conduct of private asylums in the mid-19th century (and incidentally demonstrates that Gregory's asylum was still flourishing at the same period as was Nutgrove School).[16] Richard died in 1832, unmarried, so management of the institution must have passed to another near relation.

> The most prominent case in the press during this period was that of Captain Crosbie, an inmate at Bellevue Asylum in Finglass, Dublin. Crosbie's Commission in Lunacy received vast newspaper coverage in 1859 for a number of reasons and, in many ways, initiated an extreme public interest in lunacy in the Irish press. Practically abandoned by his family, his brother living in Italy and his wife estranged from him for some months, Crosbie found himself detained in Mr. Gregory's private asylum in Finglass. This committal apparently contradicted the wishes of the Jury who were 'told and impressed with the idea that there was no intention, nor did it follow as a consequence, that Capt. Crosbie was to be shut up in a mad-house.' Their reluctance, however, does not appear to be due to any abuses, per se, in the private asylum, but more concerned with the implied deterioration of the patient's living conditions if incarcerated. Once committed, Crosbie's solicitor wrote a letter to the editor of *The Irish Times*, reporting his findings upon visiting his insane client: 'I found him confined in a small room, about 10 feet square, and about 8 feet high, with one small window and a fireplace. This room contained his bed, one chair, a small table, about two feet square on top, a basin-stand and jug,

and an old press, with a small bit of carpet before the fireplace.' While this description is obviously negative in tone, the word, 'small' recurring no less than four times, it is by no means evocative of the usual abuses and maltreatment associated with private asylum care. The solicitor proceeds, in the letter, to illustrate his client's own views:

To use his own words, he is compelled to herd with madmen. He has no books, pens, or ink allowed him; no sitting-room or place to exercise except in a courtyard some 20 yards square … and when he does walk in this yard has to submit to the threats, shouts, obscene language, and annoyances of the unfortunate creatures there assembled.

This depiction certainly contrasts with that put forward by the prominent medical men J. W. Cusack and J. T. Bankes in response to the solicitor's letter:

We have inspected the room occupied by Mr. John G. Crosbie, in the Private Asylum of Dr. Gregory, at Finglass and we consider that it is very neat, clean, and most comfortable, and suited for the care of a gentlemen [sic] in his present state of health. Large pleasure-grounds are attached to the house. From our knowledge and experience of this Asylum, we can with great satisfaction certify that it is extremely well conducted, and that the patients get a most liberal maintenance, and that they receive excellent medical treatment.

The Lunacy Inspectors also took issue with the suitability of private asylums' accommodation to the class of patient within, yet their only qualm was apparently that 'neither raiment suitable to their former position in life, nor other domestic niceties' were afforded to the lunatic. It becomes clear that what really is at issue, from both the public and medical perspective, is an alteration in accustomed living conditions. Crosbie, as the patient, complained not of his actual living arrangements, nor the medical care he received, but of the lack of amusements or occupations. He also disliked mixing with other lunatics. His solicitor concluded sardonically, 'such, Mr. Editor, are the comforts provided for Captain Crosbie, and for which his estate is to pay Dr. Gregory £100 per annum.' Thus public concern surrounding private asylums in Ireland did not focus on any abuses within the system. Indeed, it is exceptionally

> difficult to discern any abuses at all. What was at stake, however, was the 'value-for-money' afforded by private asylum accommodation and whether it would, or could, live up to the luxuries to which its higher order of patient had grown accustomed.

A typed note in the archive asserts that Anne's portrait was painted by one of the patients at Finglass. Could he have been a professional artist? It is certainly possible, given the existence of other well-known cases of artists and writers, such as Richard Dadd and Christopher Smart, being confined in private asylums during the 18th and 19th centuries. My mother thought Anne was born *c.*1750 and died *c.*1830, but her costume in the portrait suggests that it would have been painted not earlier than *c.*1820, and it shows a comparatively young woman, not someone in their 70s. I would suggest therefore that she was born *c.*1780, married *c.*1800, gave birth to Richard soon after, and had her portrait painted in her 40s. Her father, under this scenario, could have been born *c.*1750 or 1760, and would have been in his 40s or 50s when he appeared on the 1804 muster-roll.

America!

As we have seen, when Philip Jones died in 1861, his wife Mary took over the running of Nutgrove School. Her son Philip Howard William Jones (Nina's father) was born in 1862, so never knew *his* father. A silver mug, from a London maker, appears to have been a christening present. Although the hallmarks date it to 1784, it bears the inscription 'From MEH to PHWJ 1862'. We do not know the identity of 'MEH', but he or she was probably a member of the family, possibly with the surname 'Howard', as perpetuated in PHWJ's forenames. Engraved above the inscription is the boar's head associated with the Jones family, as on the bookplate illustrated earlier.

Philip H.W.Jones

One relic of PHWJ's youth survives. It is a finely crafted bronze medal contained in a handsome cedarwood box, taking the form of a Maltese cross superimposed on a laurel wreath, and with a brass roundel in the centre inscribed 'Irish Champion Bicycle Club 1881'. On the reverse the inscription reads 'Ten Miles Championship 17 Sep 1881 won by P. Jones ICBC Time 35 m 15 3/5 s'. According to Nina's accompanying note to me, this feat was achieved on a penny-farthing, so the time of well under 4 minutes per mile was impressive.

He emigrated to America at the age of 20 and worked initially for a manufacturer of agricultural machinery in Bayonne, New Jersey. Later, he joined the firm of Hays and Denton, exporters of agricultural implements, and became a well-known figure in Manhattan business circles for many years. At some point he bought a house on Staten Island, where he lived with his family for the rest of his life. According to Nina, he was 'a tall man of 6'2", had a great sense of humour, was always cheerful and loved by everyone from the boot-black boy to the boss. He was broad-minded and well read – a much-liked person for a party with his humorous stories. He had a fine baritone voice and had studied for Opera, but lack of money to continue this career sent him to New York where he became a businessman'.

He must have met his wife, Albretta Housman, soon after arriving in New York in 1882, as Nina was born in 1887. The Housman family of Staten Island had a colourful history, being closely involved in a notorious murder case in 1843, in which the chief suspect was Albretta's aunt Polly Bodine (née Housman). No possible stain from this lurid event could have touched Albretta, who was by all accounts a most kindly and respectable woman. It was her father, Captain George Housman, and his sister Polly, who were at the heart of the case.

The chief actors in the drama were related as follows:

Brothers and sister: **(Captain) George W. Housman, William Albert Housman** and **Mary (Polly) Housman Bodine.**

Mary (Polly) m. Andrew **Bodine** 1825.
Children: **Albert** b.1827;
Eliza Ann b. *circa* 1828

George W. m. 1. Emeline Van Pelt.
Child: Ann Eliza Housman (mother and child murdered 1843).

----------- m. (1847) 2. Virginia Dawson.
Children: **George W.** d. in young manhood;
Albretta.

Albretta m. Philip Jones 188?.

William Albert d.1834, aged 22.

Albretta (Housman) Jones

THE STATEN ISLAND TRAGEDY.

Murder of Mrs. Houseman and Child, by Polly Bodine.

'The Witch of Staten Island'

The best and fullest account I have found of the Staten Island murder is the following, from an anonymous blogger writing under the pseudonym 'Undine'.[17]

> On Christmas night, 1843, the holiday peace in Staten Island, NY was shattered by the sound of fire alarms. The home of sea captain George Housman had erupted in flames. The head of the household was away on a fishing trip, but remaining in the home were his wife Emeline and their baby daughter Ann Eliza. George's sister Mary 'Polly' Housman Bodine lived across the street with her father and her teenage daughter Eliza. (In 1824, Polly married an Andrew Bodine, but the marriage quickly soured, and they had been separated for many years.) When George was away, Polly would stay overnight with her sister-in-law to keep her company. This particular night, however, she was nowhere to be found. After the conflagration had been extinguished, some neighbors began investigating the damaged house.
>
> They quickly discovered a whole lot more than they had been bargaining for. The home had evidently been ransacked, with a number of valuables missing. And in

George Housman

the fire-blackened house lay the remains of Emeline and little Ann Eliza. Their skulls had been smashed, Emeline's throat was cut, and a number of their bones were broken. The poor mangled remains were scarcely recognizable as human. It was believed they had been killed the night before the blaze. This was not a tragic domestic accident, but a case of brutal murder, followed by an attempt to cover the crime with arson.

The town understandably panicked. There was a fiend on the loose. Swiftly, the whispers grew about the presumed identity of the fiend. This small, inter-related community had one suspect, and one suspect only for this unspeakably foul crime: the seemingly devoted sister-in-law, Polly Bodine.

Perhaps the greatest puzzle about this crime is the lack of any plausible motive. Polly and Emeline had always been friendly, the dead woman and her husband had no enemies, and the amount of household goods that were missing scarcely explained such a ghastly double homicide. The prosecution – despite what would prove to be nearly three years of trying – was never able to present a case that was anything more than suggestive of the accused's culpability. And yet, there was something about Polly Bodine that enabled so many who knew her to feel morally certain that she had cold-bloodedly butchered an innocent kinswoman and her year-and-a-half old child.

The local District Attorney, Lot Clark, pieced together the events of the hours leading up to the double murder. On Christmas Eve morning, Polly left Emeline's home to return to her father's residence. During that day, neighbors saw Emeline in and around her house, doing her usual chores. This proved to be the last time anyone definitely saw her alive. That evening, a woman who lived next door saw a woman she presumed was Emeline exit her home. Soon afterwards, Polly's daughter Eliza went to see if Emeline wanted anyone to spend the night. There was no answer. Eliza explained later that she assumed Emeline was spending Christmas at the home of her family, the Van Pelts.

On Christmas morning, a cousin went to Emeline's house on an errand. He repeatedly knocked on the door, but received no reply. Polly emerged from her father's house and told the boy that Emeline had gone to the Van

Pelts. She then walked off and boarded a stagecoach bound for the ferry that would take her into New York City. Polly's 16-year-old son Albert was the live-in apprentice to a Manhattan druggist, George Waite. She later claimed that she had spent all of Christmas day and night with her son and his employer, but Albert himself testified that he did not see his mother after about four p.m. On that same day, a number of items belonging to the Housmans were pawned in various shops throughout the city. All these pawnbrokers later identified the woman who brought them these household goods as Polly Bodine.

Emeline's home was silent for the rest of Christmas day. Around four in the afternoon, a neighbor riding by saw two strangers – a woman and a man in a Spanish cloak – standing in the Housmans' yard. As he passed them, the man left, while the woman entered the house. The identity of these two people remains a mystery.

The next report we have of Polly's movements is early on the morning of December 26th. A chambermaid on the Staten Island ferry saw her sitting quietly on the boat. Polly ordered a breakfast of pie and a glass of gin, which made a memorable impression on her waitress. 'I thought it marvelous that a woman would ask for gin', she recalled...

At 10 a.m. that morning, Polly was at Waite's drugstore when a Housman cousin, Freeman Smith, came to tell her of the murders. Polly – showing all the appropriate signs of shock and grief – immediately returned with him to Staten Island.

Someone else had just arrived at the Island, as well: George Housman, who was greeted with the news that his wife and child had been bludgeoned to death.

After the coroner's inquest, Polly was arrested for murder. It was claimed that her motive for this terrible crime was to steal the thousand dollars George had given his wife before he left. (The money was found still in the outhouse where Emeline had hidden it.) Polly was placed in the county jail alongside her son's employer, George Waite, who was suspected of being her accessory. On January 6th, Polly gave birth to a stillborn child. Waite was the father.

Polly went on trial on June 23, 1844. She was, to put it mildly, a controversial defendant. There was an immense, and extremely acrimonious, public interest in the case, with the citzenry hotly divided into 'She *couldn't* have done such a thing' and 'She *must* have done it' factions. Extra ferry and stagecoach runs had to be set up from as far away as New Jersey to handle the rush of spectators anxious to get even a glimpse of the woman who was becoming famed as 'The Witch of Staten Island'.

The wheels of justice did not turn smoothly during her trial. The Staten Island area was so interbred that Polly and her alleged victims were related by either blood or marriage to virtually everyone involved in the proceedings, a circumstance that guaranteed that Polly would not get an objective hearing. For some townspeople, blood ties trumped blood spilled. The most notable example was George Housman, who raised a good many eyebrows by declaring, 'I can get another wife. I can get another child. I can never get another sister.' [He did take another wife four years later – see below]. The Van Pelts and their connections, on the other hand, would have been happy to lynch the defendant on the spot. Her many rumored sexual 'sins' – most notably her long-time affair with Waite, which had caused her to undergo numerous abortions – led many to see her as a woman capable of any wickedness. For her part, Polly accused her ex-lover George Waite of the murders.

In such an emotionally-charged atmosphere, it was almost inevitable that Polly's trial ended in a hung jury. There was one holdout vote for 'innocent' – a juror who insisted that he could not vote for a conviction on circumstantial evidence unless there were four – not one, not two, not three, but four – eyewitnesses to the actual murder. He dubbed this novel bit of do-it-yourself jurisprudence 'circumstantial evidence in the fourth degree'.

It was prudently decided that 'in consequence of local and family interests, etc.', her second trial should be held outside Staten Island, and the judicial circus went on the road to Manhattan. Meanwhile, as no evidence could be found against George Waite other than his prior relationship with the accused, he was quietly released.

New Yorkers enthusiastically appreciated the new show that had landed in their midst. P.T. Barnum's Broadway museum installed a wax effigy of 'The Witch' in the act of butchering her niece and sister-in-law. This tasteful little display was immensely popular. Barnum

POLLY BODINE, ON HER RECENT TRIAL AT NEWBURG.

depicted Polly as a wizened, evil-looking old hag. The real Mrs. Bodine – a handsome woman in her mid-thirties – was outraged by this insult. Her lawyers believed she was more disturbed by Barnum's slur on her personal attractions than by any of the murder accusations. The courthouse where Polly's trial was held saw overflow crowds every day. The local papers devoted entire editions a day to the scandalous crime. Blood sells even more than sex.

Shortly before Polly's first trial, a Philadelphia paper contained a contemptuous observation by a rising young short-story writer, poet, and critic named Edgar Allan Poe: 'The trial of Polly Bodine will take place at Richmond, on Monday next, and will, no doubt, excite much interest. This woman may, possibly, escape; – for they manage these matters wretchedly in New-York.'

Poe was an excellent criminologist. Polly's second trial was an even more muddled affair than the first. A number of witnesses changed their earlier stories, and the pawnbrokers who received the silverware now professed that they were unable to identify the defendant as their customer. Despite all this, public opinion was so whipped up against the defendant that the jury had little difficulty returning a guilty verdict.

Polly's lawyers immediately appealed the verdict to the State Supreme Court. These justices agreed that the defendant had received an unfair hearing, and ordered a retrial. As a measure of her notoriety, over six thousand potential jurors had to be interviewed before the lawyers could find ten men willing to say they were unbiased about her guilt.

The lawyers for the defense were able to use this fact to obtain yet another change of venue, and the Bodine retrial wound up being held in Newburgh, New York. For all the suspicion and personal dislike Polly had inspired, there was a surprising dearth of solid evidence against her, and her attorneys were able to demolish many prosecution witnesses during cross-examination. This third jury panel, who prided themselves on being untainted by the emotional frenzy that characterized the earlier trials, very quickly acquitted her. Her first words on being found 'not guilty' were 'Can I sue Barnum now?'

The DA finally gave up the fight, and Polly Housman Bodine was safe from the law, if not from the even more merciless verdict of public opinion. Polly was virtually imprisoned by the sheer enigma of the case. To this day, no one knows why she would slaughter Emeline and her child, but on the other hand, if she didn't kill them, who did?

Polly returned home to Staten Island, where she led an increasingly reclusive life until her death in 1892. She never lived down the common belief that she was an unusually cruel murderer who had been very, very lucky. At her funeral, the only mourners were her son and daughter, who had remained devoted to her to the end. And the deaths of Emeline and Ann Eliza Housman remain forever unsolved.

To this day there continues to be a lively interest in the case, with further details being added to the picture by different researchers. In correspondence with my cousin Victor Clarendon, Marguerite M. Rivas[18] mentioned that not only were Polly and Emmeline close friends but that Polly had actually delivered the baby who was later murdered. Captain Housman was an oyster boat skipper who had, it was rumoured, recently sold a schooner and had one thousand dollars in silver hidden in his house. Polly's reputation was so toxic that the ladies of New York, when visiting the Barnum tableau, would spit on her image as they filed past. And so on. Rivas provides useful closure to the story by recording that, while George and his second wife were buried in the Moravian cemetery near the Vanderbilts, Emeline and her baby's final resting place is an untended grave overlooking a supermarket plaza, with suitably pious words still just legible on the headstone, but no mention of violent death. Polly was buried in an unmarked grave, but a century later the cemetery management erected a marker to guide the curious, who continue to seek it out.

Virginia (Dawson) Housman

A few years after the tragedy, in 1847, George Housman did indeed 'get another wife', marrying Virginia Dawson, described by Rivas as ' a wealthy blue-blooded young woman from Virginia'. She bore him several

Confederate States banknote; Alabama banknote

children, but of them only Albretta appears to have had any issue: Nina, and another girl who died in infancy, so that Nina was in effect brought up as an only child.

Virginia Housman's Southern family would probably have supported the Confederate cause in the Civil War (1861-5). Nina passed down to us an envelope containing two banknotes, nicknamed 'shinplasters', following the South's defeat which rendered them valueless. Both are dated 1864, one with a face value of $100 from 'The State of Alabama', and the other a $500 bill issued by 'The Confederate States of America'.

Our own direct link to the story is the sampler worked by Eliza Anne Bodine in 1838, in memory of her uncle Albert Housman, as described in the Prologue to this book.

(In her email, Rivas mentions that a woman in Connecticut had recently bought another sampler made by Eliza – conjuring up the picture of an obedient and industrious young girl, innocently working away at her embroidery before all these horrors broke on the family a few years later.) She was of course the daughter of Polly Bodine and has her own small walk-on part in the account of the murder given above. William Albert owned land in the Florida Keys, and also, it appears, on Staten Island, but a cryptic handwritten note attached to the back of the sampler – probably by Albretta – reads:

> Dear Nina,
>
> This William Albert Housman was your Great Great Uncle it was he that owned all at Sailor Snug Harbor he lost it and also lost his mind.

The implication, surely, is that poor Albert committed suicide in 1834 after his 'loss'. Sailors' Snug Harbor was a home for retired merchant seamen, the first in the USA, located on the north shore of Staten Island. Now designated as a National Historic Landmark District, it opened in 1833, but further research would be needed to establish the connection with Bodine.

It seems likely that, in the way of families at that time, the murdered baby Ann Eliza had been named after Eliza Ann Bodine, and Albretta after Eliza's uncle William Albert Housman. One can only imagine the traumatic effect of the murder on Eliza and her brother (also, confusingly, named Albert) of the events of 1843. Apparently neither of them ever married, and the last we hear of them is that they attended their mother Polly's funeral, held discreetly at night in 1892. To our generation, what is so extraordinary is that, far from being something that happened in the distant past, the whole saga took place a mere four generations ago, George Housman being the grandfather of my own grandmother Nina.

Eliza Ann Bodine; Albretta's cousin

Victor and Nina in New York, around the time of their marriage

Nina and Victor: courtship and marriage

On 10 June [1910 (?)] one of the New York papers carried the following story, headlined 'His Courtship Began Abroad'.

> A romance of international interest came to light today when Mr. and Mrs. Philip H.W. Jones, of 257 West Grand Street, announced the engagement of their daughter, Miss N. Virginia Gregory Jones, a choir singer of note, and Victor F. Clarendon, youngest son of Canon Clarendon, an Episcopal divine, of Belfast, Ireland. The young couple were engaged practically from the time of their first meeting in Belfast five years ago, and a month ago Mr. Clarendon came to America to ask the consent of the parents of the bride-to-be. Yesterday he sailed for home on the Lusitania, happy in the possession of Mr. and Mrs. Jones's approval of the match.
>
> Miss Jones is well known in metropolitan musical circles, having won distinction both as a concert and choir singer. She was for three years contralto [although she is listed as a soprano soloist in the programme for Elgar's oratorio 'Light of Life', performed in the German Club Rooms, Stapleton, Staten Island on 25 April 1905] in the St. Stephen's Church quartet, New York, resigning at the approach of the announcement of their engagement. Her fiancée [*sic*] is a nephew of Sir William Q. Ewart, head of William Ewart & Sons, linen manufacturers.

'Miss Nina Jones' appears on an Anchor Line 'Saloon Passenger List' for the *S.S. Columbia*, sailing from New York for Belfast and Glasgow on 15 July 1905. She and Victor became engaged in the course of a further visit to Ireland, in 1909. If the public announcement of the engagement was held back until 1910, then it seems most likely that they met in the course of the 1905 visit, as indicated by the newspaper report. They were married in 1911.

Despite their shared Irish heritage, they came from very different backgrounds. Victor, though the son of a clergyman, had the Ewart wealth behind him, and the prospect of a lucrative career in the family linen firm. Nina, only surviving child of an immigrant who was largely self-made, displays in her letters tell-tale signs of social insecurity, constantly worrying about nuances of behaviour and etiquette. As one of several such instances, she writes to her mother from Ireland:

> Strange to say I had a letter from Miss Winkler who is in the choir the most undesirable one of the lot her mother keeps a little flower stand on Spring St., N.Y. – isn't it strange how a person like that finds nerve enough to secure your address & write?

In 1909, Nina, aged 22, crossed the Atlantic to visit her Jones cousins in Ireland. The first letter home to her mother (1 July) describes an expedition to 'the invigorating air of Switzerland',

Emily Jones ('Tatters') as a girl and as a young woman

via Paris. The letter was posted from Lurgan on 3 July and stamped 'Received' at Elizabeth, New Jersey, on 9 July, impressive testimony to the speed of the ship-borne mail at that time. Enclosed with the letter is a detailed record of daily expenditure, not in her handwriting but that of her travelling companion. She does not state who this was, but the most likely candidate is her unmarried aunt 'Tatters' (Emily) as the others would scarcely have been able to abandon their families for such a jaunt. 'Tatters' lived with the family at Beech Park and helped to bring up the children.

Nina writes of the Paris fashions – 'on the whole we were disappointed at not seeing <u>any</u> extreme styles – the one I mentioned was only on a figure' – of the 'fearfully high' prices – 'they have a half dozen prices, the highest being for Americans, & they seem to think that all English speaking people are Americans!' – and of how awful Americans are (!)

> This is the only country for me I am truly ashamed to say it but America and Americans are almost loathsome to me. We met a finely dressed Southern woman & neice [*sic*] during one of our Cooks trips in Paris. They were actually chewing gum & during the drive the elder touched me on the shoulder & asked me where I got my rain-coat, then the firm & we were quite expecting the price next. Honestly it was the rudest thing I ever had to happen.

As for the French, of course their sanitary arrangements left much to be desired, and the men conformed to stereotype:

> A very rotten experience was my luck one day in our hotel – the w.c. was the size of a box with a stained glass window at the rear & high up on the left another tiny window without any glass so that if 'Gabriel blew his trumpet' the entire floor knew it! On entering the electric light went on so that anyone cd. stand outside the window & gaze upon you. The mere thought of using the place almost gave me constipation! However one day I tried it – had just arisen and was about to depart after pulling the trigger when I heard steps at the rear & on turning saw the figure of a 'black-bearded <u>froggie</u>' gazing at me. Now wasn't he a 'dirty devil'? I cd. have thrown him down the stairs but instead came forth with a stately stride & never a look to right or left & went directly to my room.

The list of daily expenditure, in francs ('25 frs to £1'), includes 'films for Kodak 5-85', 'drive in Cooks car 5-0', 'lunch on train to Montreux 4-0', 'Rigi (funicular rail) 10-50', 'entrance to Castle of Chillon 0-95' and, the most expensive purchase of all, 'lizard bag 42-0'. All these items are meticulously recorded on a sheet of headed notepaper from the Hôtel Beau Séjour (30, Boulevard Poissonière) in Paris, which offers 'Ascenseur, Bains, Eclairage Electrique, Chauffage Central'. The total cost for the whole trip, which appears to have taken about two weeks, came to £33-0s.-9d.

Succeeding letters to her mother and father feelingly describe her difficulty in adjusting to the large, and, in her eyes, rather uncouth family at Beech Park, a comfortable old house on a farm near Lurgan, Co. Armagh, owned by the Watsons. (She would have had some experience of rural life, as her father also owned a farm, at New Canaan, Connecticut.) Her aunt Mary Jones had married Hugh Watson, a solicitor, and had seven children, several of whom I remember well in their old age when Beech Park was still their base. She also spent time with her aunt Waller Jones who had married Dr Francis Crosslé and lived at Newry. Nina felt much more relaxed with this family (4 August 1909):

> ...the peace and quiet (?) of Newry is far more welcome than turbulent Beech Park. They are all genuinely fond of me here, whereas at the latter place they think it their duty to 'squelch' me and take out the small bit of confidence I have...
>
> This climate is very severe on shields [under-arm pads] & they are so vulgar at B.P. about such things that

Mary, Waller and Emily ('Tatters') as teenagers

Nina at Beech Park, photos taken by Victor

> I preferred to ask for a couple of new pairs – you see the house is a damp one and they won't dry & when I put them in the hot press once or twice & heard remarks afterward about 'stinking sweaters' & that settled it with me for I have a bit of touchy pride & decided that their vulgarity is beyond words...
>
> Don't worry, Mother dear, my 'haughty spirit' has no chance where rudeness is concerned because I am a lady thanks to your good & excellent training so that I take all insults and 'squelchings' with complete silence...
>
> Vic comes down on his motor cycle twice a week & spends the night here also the weekends which is exceedingly good of Aunt Waller.

Clearly, the young American feels completely out of her element amongst the boisterous and forthright Beech Park relations. But then, surprisingly, we are given the other side of the picture, in an earlier letter from her Aunt Mary (21 July) to her brother Philip (Nina's father) in America. This must have been passed to Nina at some point by him, and gives a robust, commonsensical view of the whole situation. All the letters from these months need to be read against the background of her 'understanding' with Victor, which became official, at least in Ireland, that summer.

> We expect your ewe lamb home today after the motor trip...Don't you worry old man, although my opinion on the subject might be biased still I recognize the fact that none of the family can grasp the fact that she is utterly different in her bringing up & all to them & there is no doubt that she has no use for girls & then Eily can't understand how she care to write & carry on with a lot of men so that's how it is. I really think it is serious between her and Vic, his mother is evidently of the opinion that it is. Of course it would seem foolish if he was an ordinary mortal, but there is lots of money there & he is a great favorite with the ruling powers his uncles & cousins & will have a soft job & plenty of money one of these days without the trouble of making it. So just you let it be an engagement. There is no doubt Vic is devoted to her & I think she is fond of him. She is looking much stronger but will never be able for any hard work. Don't be beguiled into letting her work too hard! Remember there is a lot of delicacy among the Joneses.

She and Victor had to endure the frustrations of polite socialising, when all they wanted was more time to themselves (1 July):

> The other night we behaved most beautifully but when the chance presented itself for a few words he suddenly said, 'well, I'm hanged if this isn't the greatest of cruelty to be compelled to sit in the drawing -room & talk rot as tho we saw one another quite frequently, when heaven only knows when I'll see you again after Sept.' Poor Vic, he enjoys tête-têtes [*sic*] more than 'drawing-room rot', – there, too, I'm so self-conscious and imagine that everyone has their eye on me if he sits an inch too close!

But they clearly had a lot of fun as well. Nina twice has to reassure her mother – on 23 July and 4 August – that all the motoring she is doing in Ireland is quite safe!

> Mother dear, never worry about my motoring. Vic is one of the best and most careful drivers you cd. ever want to be with – especially when I am in the car, he has often said that if ever thro his carelessness I was hurt he wd. want to leave this earth at once.

After the engagement, Nina returned home and the young couple were separated by the Atlantic ocean until they could be married two years later. None of their correspondence during this time survives, except for a mischievous postcard (27 September 1909) from Victor depicting a pair of lovers 'winding yarn' together, with a note in his handwriting:

> One of the chief advantages of the Linen Trade. The sooner I go up to Crumlin Rd Factory, the better. VFC

(The 'Factory' was where the weaving took place, the next stage on from the spinning mill.) A risky piece of banter at such a distance! – but Nina clearly took it in good part, preserving the card for the rest of her life amongst her mementoes.

A naughty postcard!

3 New York and Belfast 1911–1942

Following their marriage, Victor and Nina took a house in Belfast ('Kilcoroon', Balmoral Avenue), while Victor pursued his career at Ewart's. Their first child, Desmond, was a Leap Year Day baby, born on 29 February 1912 (the same year as my father, William Seward).

The New York Years 1914–1924

In 1914, Victor was transferred to Ewart's New York company, of which he became managing director in 1918. This would have given him valuable experience of the export side of the linen business. North and South America were the firm's major overseas markets until the 1960s, especially in tropical latitudes where the coolness of linen made it the fabric of choice, for those who could afford it. The family lived at 30 Cromwell Avenue, Dongan Hills, on the East Shore of Staten Island. My mother, Maureen, was born there, on 16 October 1915, and the youngest child, Virginia, on 31 December 1919.

Nina, Maureen and Desmond

Clockwise from top left: 30 Cromwell Avenue; on the farm: the family plus Aunt Waller; Maureen; Susan Lawther; Nina with Desmond and Maureen, M.'s christening day; Nina with Virginia

There are many photographs of the house, the children, their grandparents Philip and Albretta, and the family servant, Susan Lawther, who stayed with them for 14 years, acting as nanny and general help. There are also pictures of the family at the farm in Connecticut owned by Philip Jones. Above is a small selection.

After the birth of Virginia, in 1919, it was time to introduce the two elder children to their Irish relations. On 8 February 1920 Nina, Desmond and Maureen embarked on the 'steamer' from New York, for what was to be a lengthy trip. On Nina's return, the local newspaper reported:

DONGAN HILLS

Mrs. Victor F. Clarendon has just returned on the steamship Celtic after a trip of several months to Great Britain and Ireland. After a month in England, she was joined by Mr. Clarendon and the two motored for several weeks through the famous Highlands and other historic places in Scotland. They then went to Ireland to visit relations. Mr. Clarendon and Desmond Clarendon, who remained there, will sail for the United States on the Adriatic next week. At present Mrs. Clarendon and her two small daughters are up in the Catskill Mountains for a few weeks stay.

Nina with Desmond and Maureen, on the steamer from New York 1920

Two snapshots record their departure, both taken on deck beside the lifeboats, the first capturing Desmond and Maureen looking through a porthole.

A further newspaper clipping dated 20 August 1922 notes that Mrs Victor F. Clarendon had recently returned home from Europe, but there is no further information on this visit.

I cannot conclude this brief account of the New York years without also bringing to a close the story of Nina's beloved parents. A poignant photo of the three of them (overleaf) was taken in 1916 at The Palace Studios on the famous boardwalk at Atlantic City, New Jersey.

At this time Philip was recovering from an unnamed illness, and looks older than his 54 years. Albretta appears to be in good health, but Nina is positively blooming, with two children thriving and a third to come. Philip was to die just 5 years later, on 12 June 1921. Albretta survived him by many years and was regularly visited by her daughter and grandchildren as they grew up.

On 9 November 1923, members of the British Schools and Universities Club of New York presented Victor with a Patek Philippe gold watch, 'as a token of affection and high regard for his devoted services as its Secretary for many years'. This marked

Nina with Albretta and Philip Jones, her parents

Farewell to New York: Desmond in boater, Nina third from left, Virginia the toddler, Maureen with black socks, Albretta to her left, with glasses.

the end of his, and his family's, time in New York. Henceforth they were to live and work in Belfast, where the children grew up, went to school, and eventually married. Albretta and a number of friends came to see them off on the ship. On the back of the photo of this occasion (above), Nina notes that they had lived in New York for 10 years, so the likely date for their departure would have been early in 1924, shortly after the farewell gift of the watch. Victor became a director on the board of the parent company in April of that year.

Bexhill-on-Sea c.1924. Top: Susan Lawther and the children. Right: Maureen. Below: 'our wee car'.

Settled in Belfast, 1924–1939

The next episode in the photographic record dates to a year or so after their arrival in Belfast, when the whole family (but probably without Victor) decamped to a furnished house in Bexhill-on-Sea, Sussex for the winter. A note from Nina on the back of one of the photos taken there adds 'where I had pleurisy': why they chose Bexhill is not clear, but possibly Victor and his parents had come to know the area when he was at school in Hastings as a boy. The mystery is deepened by a snap of Maureen wearing a smart school uniform: were there thoughts of sending one or more of the children to school in Sussex? Victor's parents had spent a good deal of time in Hastings to be near Victor during his schooling.

But this was an unusual and not entirely explicable break in the normal routine of their lives. The early years back in Belfast were devoted to setting up a permanent home at 'Belhaven', 1 Deramore Park South (of which more later), and bringing up the children. As a break from the city, the family frequently visited their country connections a few miles outside Belfast: Victor's parental home at Maralin Rectory and the Watsons at Beech Park. Both were comfortable old houses with extensive grounds where Desmond, Maureen and Virginia could play and roam freely.

Top left: Thomas William Clarendon; below: Victor and TW at Maralin, 1924 Above: The Old Rectory, Maralin. Note the terrariums above and to the right of the front door.

We last encountered Victor's father, Thomas William Clarendon, when he was about to marry and enter the ministry in 1879, and his mother, Lavinia, at Christmas 1890. Lavinia died in 1913, but Thomas had progressed from being Rector of Maralin to become the Very Reverend T.W. Clarendon, Rector of Maralin and Dean of Dromore ('an Episcopal divine' in the American formulation).

Motoring loomed large as an integral part of their leisure activities. During this golden age of near-empty roads, touring must have been a real pleasure, if somewhat exposed to the elements. A note from Nina to the photograph below (passengers

The Humber

Left: Nina, Victor and Randal, early 1920s(?); Randal, Desmond and Nina, pre-1914

unidentified) reads 'The old Humber I learnt to drive. We drove in it from Derry – no top no windscreen'.

They enjoyed a variety of conveyances, including the motorcycle and sidecar (above right), a more modest vehicle which appears to be driven by Victor's elder brother Randal, complete with dog-collar. He was born in 1882, like Victor obtained an MA from Trinity College, Dublin, was ordained in 1906, and had seen service with the Royal Inniskilling Fusiliers (in France 1916-17), attaining the rank of Captain. He was always known as 'Blutey', a nickname arising from his time at Trinity: someone had said to a mutual acquaintance: 'Bring your little German friend', so he was christened 'Blücher' after the famous Prussian general who helped Wellington win the Battle of Waterloo – which finally morphed into 'Blutey'. This photograph probably predates the war, if we assume that the baby is Desmond, born 1912.

The jolliest of these motoring pictures is that showing Nina and Victor with Randal at the wheel of a splendid convertible, about to set off on some pleasure jaunt (above left). The car is left-hand drive, so probably American, and probably imported by Victor. We know that Randal never went to the US, so the photograph must have been taken in Ireland.

When contemplating the apparently unruffled tranquillity of this time, it is easy to forget that turbulent events were taking place in the wider world, and that even in the backwater of Ulster, the violence of Irish politics occasionally surfaced. In the summer of 1920, *The Belfast Telegraph* reported a Sinn Fein raid on Beech Park, headlined 'Raided Home of Sick Lady. Two Rifles Prize of "Daring"'. The perpetrators come across as slightly amateurish, but even so it must have been a frightening experience for the family and servants, occurring as it did during the turmoil of the Irish War of Independence (1919-21). While most of the fighting was south and west of what came to be the border, Ulster was by no means unaffected. Here is the report.

A party of 20 Sinn Feiners attended Lurgan Show yesterday on bicycles. They enjoyed the show during the day, and no comment was passed on their presence. About 4.30 o'clock they left singly and in twos and threes and proceeded to the residence of Mrs. Watson, Beechpark, about one mile from Lurgan, in the County Down. They forcibly entered the house, and stole several rifles from it. After leaving the premises the men dispersed in all directions, and no trace as to their whereabouts has up to the present been found.

> ...Beechpark House is situated in its own grounds...on the Dromore Road. It is approached by an avenue which sweeps to the house, and is bounded on both sides by thick timber, which completely conceals the house from the road.
>
> The residents of Beechpark were at Lurgan Show, with the exception of Mrs. Hugh Watson, who was seriously ill in charge of a nurse. The only other people in the house were a man-servant and maid. The man-servant has only been in Mrs. Watson's employment for two months, and on hearing a knock at the door opened it, to see a crowd of armed men facing him. They demanded entrance and filed in, completely filling the spacious porch.
>
> They demanded from the man-servant where the rifles were. He said he did not know of any rifles, as he was only there a short time. Meanwhile Mrs. Watson's nurse turned up, and, appreciating the situation, she told the raiders of Mrs. Watson's illness. They then said if they did not find the rifles they would return and shoot the man-servant. They searched the house and secured two rifles and some ammunition.
>
> Before the war a company of Ulster Volunteers drilled at Beechpark, and admittedly kept their arms there. Shortly after the war broke out the arms were handed over to the Government.
>
> Mr. Henry Watson...said he was not prepared to say how many rifles had been taken, but that both rifles and ammunition were missing. He turned up at the house five minutes after the raiders had left, to find everything in disorder. He immediately informed the Lurgan police and left the matter in their hands.

Growing up and school in Ireland

After early schooling in Belfast, Desmond attended Campbell College, described by C.S. Lewis, who spent one term there, as having 'been founded for the express purpose of giving Ulster boys all the advantages of a public school education without the trouble of crossing the Irish Sea'.[19] He proceeded from there to Worcester College, Oxford, the first in the family to go to Oxbridge rather than to Trinity College, Dublin. He may have invited Maureen, then aged 18, to join him there in 1934 for the end-of-year festivities, as she kept amongst her souvenirs the dance cards for Commemoration Balls at St John's and New Colleges. These are adorned with ribbons in the college colours, with little pencils attached for the ladies to note down their partners ('Engagements') for each dance. There are a mixture of waltzes ('You have taken my heart') and foxtrots, some of them popular hits ('It don't mean a thing') and some jazz numbers ('Bugle Call Rag', 'Xmas Night in Harlem'). There were three Supper breaks, the last at 2 a.m., and a photograph at 6 a.m. Music at New College was provided by The Casani Club Orchestra, directed by Charles Kunz, later to achieve fame and popularity as pianist 'Charlie Kunz': in fact he made his debut as a soloist the same year. If she indeed went to both balls she must have had some stamina, as they were on successive nights, 19 and 20 June.

(In the 1980s, during my time as an editor at Batsford, one of my authors was Asa Briggs, the Provost of Worcester College. I was working with him on the third book in his Victorian trilogy, *Victorian Things*. He invited me to stay with him and his wife Susan at the Provost's Lodge, treated me to dinner at High Table, and personally brought me a cup of tea in bed the next morning. He was the most dynamic person I have ever met, truly a one-man industry, and utterly without pretension.)

By 1931, both Maureen and Virginia were pupils at Hillcourt School, Glenageary, Dublin, when they appear in a school photograph, aged respectively 15 and 11. It appears that there were only about 50 girls in the whole school, so it was very select. The photo overleaf features in a nicely produced souvenir album which also includes shots of the house itself, the hallway, the lodge with sweeping drive curving off into the trees, and one of the girls' dormitories. The latter is as homely as could be, with flowered wallpaper and fabrics, cuddly toys on the bed, and photos of film stars on the shelf above. How very different from the Spartan accommodation provided in most boarding schools

at this period and for many decades afterwards!

Like most girls of her age, Maureen was an avid collector of cigarette cards and autographs of film stars and sporting heroes. However, her most notable acquisition was the signature of W.B. Yeats (1865-1939) with accompanying verse, in her autograph book. One of her fellow-pupils, though four years younger, was Yeats's daughter Anne (she of 'A Prayer for My Daughter'), who later became a noted painter and stage designer (1919-2001). The verse – sadly not fresh-minted for the occasion – is the chorus from his well-known early poem 'The Stolen Child' (1889).

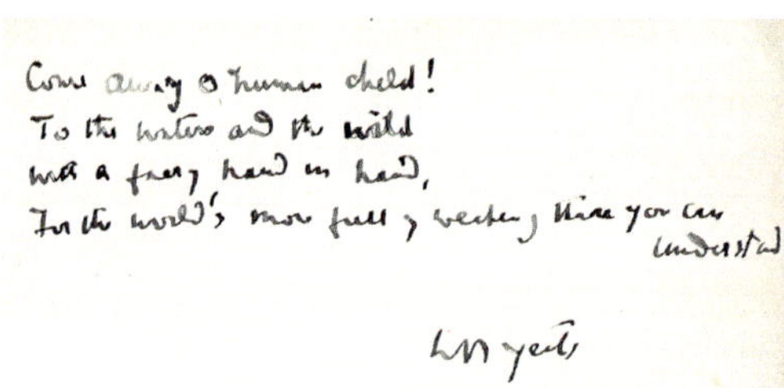

Come away, O human child!
To the waters and the wild
With a faery, hand in hand,
For the world's more
full of weeping than
you can understand.

From Hillcourt, Virginia was sent away to Sherborne Girls' School in Dorset, while Maureen stayed on until the end of her schooling, when she returned to Belfast.

Life back at home with her parents was good. Her letters and photographs through the 1930s evoke a relatively carefree world of tennis parties, dances, boyfriends, and holidays with friends and relations. One of these was a caravan jaunt around the West of Ireland, another a sailing holiday on the Norfolk Broads. Motor racing was a great enthusiasm and there are several references to attending meetings, including a press pass she somehow obtained for the Limerick Grand Prix of 1936, inscribed in pencil on the back 'Miss M.C. Clarendon chief sob sister' (from someone for whom she had been a confidante?). Occasionally, she would travel with Nina to the US to visit her grandmother, on one memorable voyage playing deck quoits with Oscar

Hammerstein. Her passport for the1930s bears temporary visas for two such visits: the first for 40 days from 2 October 1933, and the second for 60 days from 6 October 1936.

But the most fully documented experience was that of staying with a German family in Freiburg. This was an extended visit of four months, from February to May 1938. The only hint in her letters that anything was amiss, only 18 months before the outbreak of war, is a reference to 'verdunkeln' – a night of total blackout which she thought was connected to 'some kind of aeroplane practice'. She was a paying guest in the household of a retired Doctor Wack and his wife, who fed her well and looked after her assiduously when she became ill with mumps. Virginia was staying with another family in Freiburg. The serious purpose of the stay was to improve their German, and their singing (and their skiing!), but there was plenty of time outside lessons to explore the surrounding countryside and to socialise with young German men. One, Hans Gunter, Frau Wack's son by her first marriage, was particularly admired. He had returned after a three-month skiing trip to America after graduating from Munich University, and subsequently went on to work in the research department of an artificial silk factory.

Nina visited the girls during this time, followed later by Victor. He arrived in Freiburg on Tuesday 15 March and four days later whisked Maureen off on a tour of Switzerland and Northern Italy, arriving in Venice on 27 March. They spent only two full days there, staying at the famous old Grand Hotel Danieli, close to Piazza San Marco. They visited the glass works on the island of Murano and the Lace School on Burano. Maureen was clearly impressed by the latter, giving a detailed description of how each of the pillow lace workers specialised in a certain stitch, dividing up the design between them: she purchased a fine d'oyly depicting a hunting scene, and two butterflies.

Burano Lace School

> About 60 girls all working away. They do simply wonderful work – the finest I have ever seen. We bought a small d'oyly for putting underneath a finger bowl, for 8/-. It would take one girl two weeks to make it! But they all specialise each in a different stitch, so when one girl

Burano lace: a hunting scene

has done her special stitch in the pattern, it is passed on to another to do a different stitch in another part of the pattern, & so on and so on until it is finished.

From Venice they sailed down the Adriatic on the Italian ship *Paganini*, whose captain fell in love with Maureen, and pursued her with letters and postcards after she had returned to Freiburg ('poor man he is in a bad way!', she commented). He was trying to persuade her to rejoin the ship at Genoa and so to Marseilles on her way back to Ireland, which 'would be marvellous but would cost so much more!'. Eventually she lost patience with him (though she kept one letter and a postcard), writing to her father on 9 May,

> The captain is beginning to get on my nerves a bit – he has written 3 letters & two postcards to my one letter! What does he expect anyway, I will probably never see him again, more than likely in fact.

At some point, probably when the ship called at Ancona or Bari, she parted from the cruise and returned to Freiburg, while Victor continued to Catania, Malta and then on to London, arriving on 14 April.

She was back in Freiburg by mid-April for several more weeks of German and singing lessons, motoring trips and evenings with friends in the town – including a visit to the cinema to see a 'marvellous picture' of the 1936 Berlin Olympics (the notorious classic directed by Leni Riefenstahl, presumably). There is a jolly postcard of the 'Weinstube Briem' (just one block away from Adolf Hitler Strasse), sent to Belfast after her return by one of the group – 'the wine in the old Briem is still the best'. She and Virginia hatched a plan to stay in Paris on the way home, but Victor would only allow this if it did not cost too much and a 'reliable person' could be found to show them round: apparently, it was not expected that two young women of 22 and 19 would be capable of working out what 'sights' to see for themselves – or perhaps this concern simply masked a more serious worry that they might come to some harm in the big city. In any case they spoke no French, so in the end agreed that it had not been such a good idea after all.

They left Freiburg on 1 June, stopping in London for a day or two before returning to Belfast. So ended a remarkable sojourn abroad which must have been a formative experience for both Maureen and Virginia, opening their eyes to the wider world outside Ireland. They saw a good deal of Germany and Austria, mixed with several nationalities, learned some German and improved their singing, but above all enjoyed a certain degree of independence. Maureen's letters are full of enthusiasm for it all and, one senses, a growing confidence in herself. It seems curious that she writes to her mother and father separately, but they were both busy people, Nina leading a hectic social life and Victor often away on business: nowadays they would be one of those couples who have to keep in touch by email, even though living under the same roof. While reticent on some matters, they are all surprisingly frank about others, and their personalities, likes and dislikes come through with great vividness.

Love and war, 1939–1942

War came. The young men dispersed across the UK and overseas, writing forlorn letters from wherever they happened to be posted. 'This is about my last from England', wrote Stephen Boycott from Norfolk on 12 November 1939. He was with the 3rd Searchlight Regiment, Royal Artillery; his next extant letter, a year later from base on Salisbury Plain, mentions casually 'a man I met when I got back from Dunkirk' – how much he must have seen and experienced in that short time. In his last letter, from 20 January 1942, he is very bucked that he, three other officers and two NCOs from the regiment were 'mentioned in despatches for the Dunkirk show...So getting wounded in the behind does seem to have been some use after all.' Private Douglas Badham writes from Castlerock, Co. Derry, on 10 October 1940, that it's a dump, but enlivened by his participation in the regimental dance band. Home for him is Oxford, where his family are 'all busy canteening' as part of the war effort. Maureen at this stage was also helping out in some capacity: 'Now you can get back to your darling children, or is it the soldiers' turn today? I hope you never get your mind mixed up between the two.'

Her most regular correspondent at this time, however, was Neil Daly from Montenotte, Cork. A hard-drinking, hard-riding solicitor – and seemingly a confirmed bachelor – he was a friend of her closest school pal, Jean, who married John Elmes. The detailed chronicle of hunting, fishing, horse races, rounds of golf

Stephen Boycott with Virginia, Maureen and Nina at 'Belhaven', 1940

and parties becomes repetitive, but there are interesting insights into the uncomfortable dilemma faced by the Southern Anglo-Irish, who had until so recently been British citizens. On 12 November 1940 he writes:

> Well, Maureen, I'm sorry, personally, that you can't have our ports. Particularly as, – I think I gave you a lecture on the matter, – I know or think I know something of their importance...However, if 'Dev' [Eamonn De Valera, the Irish president] is going to stick to his idea of keeping us neutral (on which question I offer no opinion, as, speaking from a purely national ('Eire' national) point of view – and we are of course a nation-, it is at least a very difficult one) he can't of course lend lease or give them either to you or to Hitler.
>
> From a practical point of view, I may tell you that if he did ...it would just give the extreme and even the only partly extreme 'Ireeshan' crowd here exactly one right kind of excuse to create general hell of a type that is now mercifully dead.
>
> Of course we stink now in your nostrils, but I see no easy cure.

On 17 May 1941 he writes that he is 'very horrified to read of the pretty awful plasterings you've got from the bombers, and indeed have got fairly shattering reports of it from people who've come down – much more serious than what the papers say...I'm assuming you're safe & well, but why I don't know.' There had in fact been a series of devastating air raids in April and May, for which Belfast was quite unprepared, the authorities assuming that the city was beyond the range of the Luftwaffe. 3,200 houses were destroyed, and the docks and industrial base severely damaged: there is a melancholy photograph of the looms at Ewart's blackened, burned and entirely open to the sky.

The carefree pre-war life had come to an abrupt end. Although the dancing and socialising continued, it was now on a wartime footing, members of the armed forces returning from leave to snatch whatever rest and recreation they could. In many ways this was a positive development, as it introduced fresh cohorts of young men and women to the social mix. Maureen went to work, initially in the officers' canteen at the docks. This may have been on a voluntary basis, but later on she took what was probably her first, and was definitely her last, paid employment, working in the censor's office. Virginia joined the WAAF and was posted to different parts of the UK as time went on. Desmond had moved to the New York office of Ewart's in 1938, and joined the Canadian army; later he was posted back to the UK and, in the last stages of the war, to Italy.

Maureen's work at the officers' canteen was the means by which she met my father, Lieutenant W.R. Seward, RNVR – 'Bill'. He was on convoy duty in the North Atlantic, captaining a corvette, and found a loving home-from-home at 'Belhaven', where the family looked after him when he was on leave or ill. His naval adventures are for a later chapter. Here, we merely record the fact that he and Maureen fell in love, became engaged in 1941, and married in Belfast on 4 March 1942.

Letters of congratulation came in from friends, relations, from Bill's sister Dorothy, and even – they being decent chaps – from disappointed former boyfriends. The most entertaining and affectionate was from an elderly cousin, the distinguished retired surgeon Wyclif McCready, from his farm at Ballymacarron, Toye, Co. Down, on the west shore of Strangford Lough. He was another Ewart descendant, without whose researches writing this memoir would have been infinitely harder. In 1929 he published an enormously detailed family tree, or 'genealogical table' of the Ewart family[20], giving dates, qualifications, careers, marriages, and honours of the whole clan up to that date. Here is perhaps the place to pay due honour to his shade. From his own entry on the table we learn that he was born in 1880, gained his BA from Trinity College Dublin, qualified MB, FRCSI, was Surgeon, Belfast Ophthalmic Hospital; Captain 10th Battalion Royal Irish Rifles and RAMC; mentioned in despatches; married 1917 Ellen Workman of Glasgow. To us, Ellen was 'Cousin Nellie' and he 'Old Wic', their son being 'Young Wic'. Our visits to Belfast always included calling in for tea at the farm, where we were entertained by Nellie and her daughter-in-law Margaret (another Scottish girl) who by this stage largely ran the farm while Young Wic worked during the week in Belfast. We generally walked through the fields and along the shore of the lough; it was a beautiful place, and the lough and its surroundings are now an internationally important wildlife reserve.

> Oct.22.1941
>
> My dear Maureen,
>
> We must stop taking in the Whig [*The Northern Whig*, a liberal unionist newspaper], because it doesn't seem to have the really important news in it.
> ...You may wonder then why my poor words of congratulation have been so long delayed & may naturally be contemptuous when I tell you I have for three days been much concerned with the trivial work of threshing...
>
> Both Nellie and I took to him [Bill] at once & as for you, my mind was made up years ago when you just turned up at College Gardens with a gaping mastoid which I had to dress & you were a really affectionate good little thing...perhaps when your sea-rover comes back to Belfast now and again to replenish his ship with beeves and flour you will find petrol to come down here.
>
> It is as good a place for courting as any I know and I <u>do</u> know, for there is an old doll down here that I have been courting for years & years – and the game still goes on.
>
> ...I hope the Ginger one [Virginia] is well & hearty & finds the salvation of her country a job to her liking.
>
> Give her my love & give it to yourself too & the honoured one you might greet in some way that seems most suitable & tell him there is always a welcome for him & his at the house of
>
> Your very affectionate cousin
>
> W McCready

This completes the account of my mother's origins and progress, until her meeting and marriage to my father. We will return to Northern Ireland to trace its continuing significance for my parents' and my own generation, but it is now time to shift the focus from Ireland and America to England, and the Sewards.

4 Seafaring, Emigration and Railways: The Seward Family 1795-1900

Prisoner of the French: John Rendell

From 1793 Britain was at war with Revolutionary France, a conflict which touched almost every family in the country. The earliest letters in the Seward archive date from March 1795 and are from a mariner, John Rendell of West Teignmouth in Devon, who was incarcerated as a prisoner of war in a former convent in Quimper, Brittany. There is no record of how he was captured, but he had drawn up his last will and testament on 8 May 1794, possibly in anticipation of the voyage which ended so disastrously for him,

> ...being about to proceed to sea and knowing the casualties and dangers incident thereto and knowing the uncertainty of life...

This will was to be the cause of much dispute within the family later, our copy being annotated by a later Seward: '...my Uncle John Rendell's Will...I never received a Farthing of what was given under this Will. W.J.Seward'.

There are two letters, one to his mother Sarah Rendell, and the second to his sister, also Sarah (1765-1843), who was married to another mariner, William Seward. They give a graphic account of John's sufferings and loneliness. It appears all too likely that he did not survive the experience, died unmarried, and left no direct descendants. He wrote first to his mother on 2 March, but the letter is in poor condition, with two fragments missing. However, it is possible to make out that he wishes her to receive the balance of the £100 Mr Brake of Exeter had insured for him, after some other calls on it, then to pay herself and put the rest in the bank. He moves on to a description of the conditions endured by himself and his fellow-prisoners ('...' indicates missing or illegible words or phrases):

> I would not wish my Dear Mother should...our real

> situation it would almost break her heart...only say this that Upwards of sixteen Hundred People has died ...starv'd which caused a dreadful fever to rage & that we have had nothing but bread &water servd out to us this month past. Our situation is realy pityful when we first came here, here was over four thousand people but near one half has been starvd to Death for want of Common Necessarys to support them. The Unhuman Beings have taken most everything from us all. Some have scarce Cloathes enough to cover their Nakedness & then to be drove into a Prison to be starvd with Cold & Hunger. How I am to go through this next summer I cannot tell but must trust in my God for soon to be delivered as we have now great talk of Peace soon taking place which will be welcome News to many. I hope my Dear Mother recd my letter I sent by Lady Fitzroy who was a Prisoner here...William Charles Price is well & desires his Compts to all.

As a PS he mentions officers known to his correspondents, some dead, one with him in the prison, others missing.

The letter to his sister is dated 17 March, and provides further details of his situation. He might well have died on the anticipated forced march to Paris, to which he alludes here.

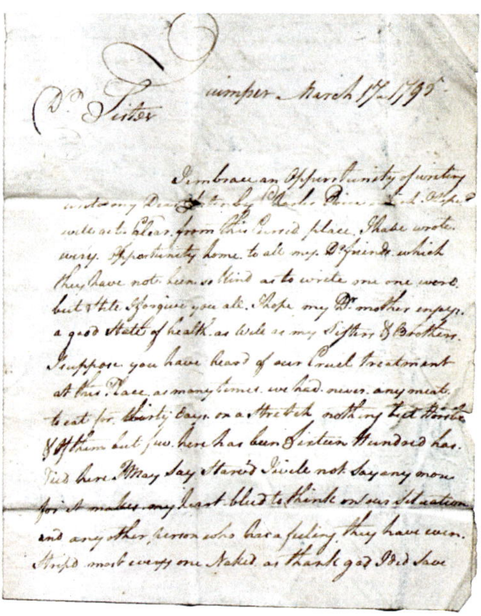

First page of John Rendell's letter to his sister

> I embrace an Opportunity of writing unto my Dear Sister by Charles Price which I hope will get Clear from this Cursed place. I have wrote every Opportunity home to all my Dr friends which they have not been so kind as to write me one word but I forgive you all. I hope my Dr mother enjoys a good state of health as well as my Sisters & Brothers. I suppose you have heard of our Cruel treatment at this Place as many times we had never any meat to eat for thirty days on a Stretch nothing but ... & of them but few. Here has been Sixteen Hundred has died here I may say starved I will not say any more for it makes my heart bleed to think on our

situation and any other person who has a feeling. They have even stripd most everyone naked as thank god I did save a few things by remaining at Brest Hospital where I was Ill there two months but I thank god I got the Better of it and are still in good health god be praised. It will be past the Art of the greatest genius to paint our real situation past but now it is a little better. I have obtained my parole to live in the town by paying for my own Board but god knows how long we are to remain here I cannot tell for they are now marching of Prisoners from here towards Paris which from 50 to 60 days march for us but god knows how I am to withstand the Journey I cannot tell & we are sure to loose every thing but what we stand in which at Present is not a great Deal. I wrote Sister before desiring her to call on Mr Brake to see if he has ... my Insurance & how she was to do with it & likewise Dear Mother about three weeks since. I hope soon to receive a letter from you as if possible I shall remain here. I must bid you all adieu do give my Duty to my Dr Mother & love unto my Dr Sisters & Brothers & William & the same attend yourself. From your ever affectionate Brother

J Rendell

I hope you have heard from Brother soon after my Departure they person who ow'd him the money died here in Prison ... Capt. West [of Teignmouth] marched from here three months since & several of ...since died. ... is well. Remember me to my old friend S Langley & tell him I have wrote him several letters & remember me to all the girls they are happy & I am fretting

Adieu

Unfortunate
You write direct for me Rendell
Prisoner of war Quimper
Brittany

Remember this is my birthday

His account of the horrors of Quimper is corroborated by other reports which began to trickle back to England at this time (note the tribute to Lady Fitzroy, referred to in John's first letter). The following is taken from the BBC's 'History Extra' website.

'It would make your heart ache to see our poor sailors, without money, without clothes, worn down by sickness and emaciated to the last degree, fighting over the body of a dead dog, which they sometimes pick up and devour with the most voracious appetite,' wrote one prisoner in 1795. This letter made it to England and was published in the newspapers. 'I am the only surviving midshipman of four', he added, 'I have lost all my hair by sickness but I live in hopes of seeing Old England and my friends again.'

Those who made it home also carried accounts of terrible conditions. One such man was a Liverpudlian shipwright who managed to escape from the prison in 1794 with six others. They sailed across the Channel in a stolen boat using their shirts to construct a makeshift sail, finally landing at Sidmouth in Devon.

Winston Graham used first-person reports of Quimper prison when researching the *Poldark* novels. In *Poldark's Cornwall* – a companion to the *Poldark* novels – Graham recalls using a letter by one Lady Anne Fitzroy which outlined the conditions at Quimper. Sister of Arthur Wellesley, Duke of Wellington, Lady Anne Fitzroy had been incarcerated at Quimper for around nine months, after a boat on which she was travelling from Lisbon was captured by the French near Falmouth.

On account of her sex, she was given different accommodation from the rest of the prison population and was kept under guard at a house in the convent's grounds. Contemporary reports, however, suggest that despite being better treated than others, Lady Anne Fitzroy worked fearlessly to improve the conditions of the prisoners, sourcing medicines, buying food, petitioning the French, and sending letters home to England to raise awareness of their fate. One prisoner later wrote in his memoirs: 'her benevolence was unbounded [and] through her goodness and humanity the lives of more than three thousand poor distressed objects were preserved… She was, to us, a second Moses.'[21]

The story of John's hardships sets the scene for much of what follows in succeeding generations: a strong connection with the sea, hard working lives, money worries, and little time to enjoy the refinements of life that were so abundantly available to the Ewarts and Clarendons. It is nonetheless an inspiring story, each generation becoming slightly more prosperous than the last and gradually moving up the social scale, until by the end of the nineteenth century, the sons at least were able to benefit from a good education and to become more securely established in the professional and managerial classes. This steady progress is mirrored in a gradual improvement in the style and literacy of their written communications.

The remainder of this chapter covers the four generations preceding the birth of my grandfather William Thomas Renell Seward in 1880. For the Seward family tree, see Appendix 1, p.134.

Four generations

1. William Seward (d.1815), master mariner

The earliest papers following John Rendell's letters from Quimper are a group of four documents[22], from the early 1800s, concerning damage to two ships of which William Seward, John's brother-in-law, was Master. He died in 1815, his widow Sarah living on until 1843.

It is likely that all four documents were drawn up in support of insurance claims. The first, dated 3 November 1804, is a statement 'sworn on the Holy Evangalist' before the British vice-consul in Lisbon. It is a survey conducted by a shipwright, a sailmaker and two mariners and shipmasters, who were present in the port at the time and went on board the brigantine *Good Intent* to assess storm damage 'as well as circumstances would permit (she having a cargo of fish onboard)'. The damage was as follows:

> The Jib Boom, the Starboard Bow rail and the Larboard Quarter Boards gone. The Starboard Quarter Rail and Stanchions and the Quarter Boards broken and rendered unserviceable the Bolts and Seams strained and they found also a deficiency of fish in the cargo which they suppose had been thrown overboard for the general Preservation and these Appearers further declared that the said Brigantine must be caulked and all the other damages repaired and replaced and made good without which she cannot proceed to sea.

The second, from September 1810, is headed 'Memorandum of Occurrance as happened on board the Brig *Good Intent* of Teignmouth, William Seward, Master, on the Prosecution of his voyage from Liverpool to St John's, Newfoundland'. The *Good*

Intent 'then being tight, staunch and strong' left Liverpool on 11 September with a cargo of coals and coke. On 14th it departed from Inishtrahull, a small island off Co. Donegal, about 10 kilometres north-east of Malin Head. Nothing of note happened during the early part of the voyage but then they encountered contrary winds and gales until 8 October, when in a strong gale 'with thick rain and very dark...in the act of reefing the fore and aft Mainsail to our very great surprise our vessel struck against another.' There follows a vivid description of the consequences of this collision.

> ...a strange voice told us that the vessel was sinking and the Master and Mate was overboard. To our Bows, our people being forward, said our vessel was sinking, for our Bows was quite open and water flowing in. I ordered the pumps to work. To our satisfaction they soon sounded. The people in the meantime doing all in our power to save the two men overboard. With difficulty the Mate was saved, but the Master being entangled in the ropes, could not get him inboard and he perished...[at] daylight...we saw the schooner to windward, which bore down and kept with us. It still blowing fresh with thick rain, our vessel making a good deal of water, obliged us to keep our pump always at work. The oakum washing out of the wooden ends. We considered how to stop the pumps and cut away the wreck of the stem. In the doing of which our Mate was washed from the Bows and drowned...On Tuesday Ninth little wind...Hoisted out the boat and took the Mate and Man onboard the American Schooner. Their late Master John Geary from Gothenburg to Marvelhead [probably Marblehead, Mass.] loaded with hemp and iron out 48 days.

After further bad weather and damage to the ship she finally arrived safe at St John's on 22 October. It is not clear what happened to the American schooner – perhaps it was abandoned once the mate and man had been taken off, if there were no other crew members.

The third and fourth are dated 16 and 20 October 1814 and are once again sworn statements made before the British vice-consul in Lisbon, the former being an account of what had happened, by William Seward, Master, and the Mate and Seaman on the schooner *Jubilee*; and the latter a survey in the same format as the earlier example from 1804. These statements of the charges and damages sustained on the voyage were obtained for the benefit of anyone with an interest 'in the said schooner *Jubilee* or her cargo'. The ship had sailed on 22 September from St John's, Newfoundland with a cargo of dried cod. Interestingly, it was 'under convoy of His Majesty's Sloop of War *Prometheus*', which suggests that it needed protection – from what? Although the French and Spanish navies had been neutralised at Trafalgar in 1805, some French ships were able to break the British blockade. A further hazard was hostility from American ships during the War of 1812, which did not end until early in 1815 (see Appendix 2, p.136).

Once again, the vessel was the victim of fierce storms, at one point reaching hurricane force. In an effort to save the ship and crew it was decided to throw some of the cargo overboard; accordingly, they 'began to take fish from the after hold and pass up the Companion as soon as possible'. During a lull they 'saw the *Prometheus* laying to within a gunshot on their weather quarter' and another ship dismasted. They may have lost contact with the convoy, as the *Prometheus* 'bore up and made sail without making any signal'. However, after enduring further strong gales and unsettled weather, they reached Lisbon safely on 15 October. Again, the damage was considerable, the ship 'apparently strained all over'. The 'Appearers' were able to confirm this and 'upon examining into the After Hold ...[observed] therein a vacancy that might have contained one hundred Quintal of fish which was thrown overboard at sea for the General Preservation'.

2. *William John Seward (1791-1858), master of an emigrants' depot*

William John Seward, son of William the master mariner, was trained as a cabinet maker but at some point became Master of the Emigrants' Depot at Plymouth. He married four times, his third wife being Ann Rendall (d.1830). Their eldest son was William Rendall Seward (1816-1884), who married Charlotte Poe Renell Gough (1811-1897). (All these Rendalls, Renells and Rendles are confusing but are probably just variant spellings of the same name.) The fourth wife was Mary, who died in 1861, and whose will was the cause of another vitriolic family dispute.

The Emigrants' Depot was one of several established around the country to deal with the mid-century waves of emigration, mainly from Scotland and Ireland but also from England.[23] There were more emigrants from Devon and Cornwall than from any other counties, so Plymouth was well placed to receive them. Hitherto, the most popular (and cheapest) destination had been North America, but the government, in an effort to divert some of this flow to the more distant colonies, created the Colonial Land and Emigration Commission in 1840. The Commissioners acted as agents for the colonial governments of the Cape, Australia and New Zealand, who sold land and used the proceeds to assist passengers to these destinations. The first depots to collect the emigrants before embarkation were established by private contractors at Deptford and Plymouth.

At Plymouth, storehouses on Elphinstone Wharf were converted in 1847 for use as a depot. (There must have been a depot in existence before that, however, as from WJ's 1842 letter below it is clear that he was by then already fully involved in providing accommodation for emigrants.) Constructed at the height of the potato famine, it soon became the collection point for thousands of Irish emigrants, escaping from desperate poverty at home. They embarked on weekly steamers from towns such as Cork, Waterford and Dublin, arriving in Plymouth to await the next emigrant ship to call in. None of the ships started from there, instead using London or Southampton as their base ports. Picking up the emigrants from Plymouth had several advantages: it was already on the western side of the country, it allowed the ships to load cargoes of goods at the base port, and meant that the emigrants (and the governments providing them with assisted passages) did not have to incur the additional expense of travelling to London, or the frequent hazards of sailing down the English Channel.

In a debate in Parliament (Hansard 6 April 1854) it was stated that the steamers from Ireland were so crowded and insanitary that emigrants frequently suffered more on the passage across the Irish Sea than on the long voyage to Australia. Already debilitated by poor living conditions at home, many arrived in Plymouth with wounds or infection caught on the journey; some died. The depot was well equipped to deal with the situation, isolating the sick and providing appropriate medical attention. As a result, the mortality rate was far lower than in the town of Plymouth itself when epidemics broke out.

The depot could accommodate up to 500 emigrants, who often had to wait several weeks for their passage, which had been booked in advance. They were met at the train station or the dock by depot servants and escorted to the accommodation that had been allocated to them. In 1849 the South Devon Railway opened a line as far as Millbay Station, so that emigrants from the North could now reach Plymouth via the Bristol and Exeter Railway. The rapid development of the local railway network at this time is described in WJ's letter of 11 December 1846:

> [In the summer] I will try to come up to London as my governor contracts with the company for the conveyance of his people up and down our railroad from Plymouth to Exeter. The South Devon line goes on very rapid and they are going to Parliament to get a Central Line in connexion with the South Western line and the directors on that line are going to join in connexion with the Sutton Pool company here to make Docks &Wharves for the convenience of ships landing their passengers and light cargoes instead of taking them to London as it will be much cheaper to convey them by rail than for the ships to go to London. It will be a great saving in time & expence.

William John's letters to his son William in London (who was pursuing a career on the railways), give many detailed insights into the day-to-day business of managing the Depot, and the sheer scale of the operation. We know from other sources, for example, that in 1848, 89 ships sailed from Plymouth carrying 8,505 emigrants; and in 1849, 130 ships with 15,895 emigrants, of which 109 (14,118 emigrants) were destined for Australia and 10 (1,171 emigrants) for Canada. The two letters below make it clear that he was managing it on behalf of the owners, who might change from time to time according to their own fortunes. 'Your Grandmother' is the widow of W.J.'s father; Hadassah, Betsey, Susan and Henry are young William's sisters and brother; Charlotte his wife. Henry was always to be a problem, finding it difficult to hold down a job, until he eventually emigrated to Australia with his wife and children the year after his father's death in 1858. On 8 May 1842 WJ writes:

> ...I suppose you have heard of my removal to Plymouth. How long I shall remain here is uncertain. I rather expected last year either to be sent to Gravesend or Dublin but as there is nothing doing this year of any consequence in the Emigration line I remain here. Our salary is now very low in consequence of it but we expect it will recommence next year with fresh vigour. Ours is a very trying life. I had no less this time 12 months at a time in the house than 400 to 600 Irish Emigrants for whom I provide Breakfast, Dinner & Supper with a Bed, and I have had

> some of them more than 3 months with me. They are a curious people to do with. My establishment then belong to Mr Marshall 25 Birch Lane but in consequence of the Money Markets in Australia being in such a depressed state he was oblidged to suspend his payments, and my place was transferred over to the present Lord Mayor of London but I heard yesterday that Mr Marshall's affairs will pay 20 Shillings in the pound so that I shall be transferred over to him again. Your Grandmother is still living at Teignmouth. I allow her 2/- per week. I heard from her last week she is as well as ever she is now in her 78 year. Hadassah was married here at Plymouth to Mr Webber the Carver (I suppose you remember him) last September he is rather older than she but I am confident will make a kind and affectionate Partner to her and I trust that she will do the same for him. Henry is still with me. He would go to Sea. I fitted him out with necessarys for the Voyage which cost me nearly 7£. He went to Newfoundland was absent about 3 months and when he came home he had lost the greater part of his ... Clothes and would not go to Sea any more. He is now learning the Trade of a Joiner & he must be bound for 5 years and to receive no wages until he has served half his time it seems that is the custom of this place. He seems to get on with this. Susan is oblidged to be sent into Cornwall to try the change of air she has never recovered the effects of that fit of Illness she had at London. I put her to School but it affected her health so much that she is oblidged to leave it off [she died on 23 November 1846]. I trust you will let me hear from you once more if I cannot see you and also if you know where Betsey is do let me know for I assure you there is nothing would give me greater pleasure than to hear from you kind love to Betsey should you see her my kind love to Charlotte and I remain your affectionate but forgotten Father
>
> W J Seward

and on 27 June 1854:

> ... I wish my dear William I could see you. I have various schemes in my head but as yet the way to bring them out seems edged up, but I trust before long brighter views may await you. We are very busy here at present. I only wish your Brother [Henry] could write like you what a help he would be to me. He does the same on board the ships as I

> expect your Uncle does [keeping the ships' lists and accounts]. He does it for Mr Foulds who holds the same office here as Mr Chant does in Liverpool, but Henry has not anything to do with any writing.
>
> I hope before long I shall be able to walk about again when I will make enquiries among the railway officials if any thing can be done on this line for you. Webber's Brother has the looking after the Electric Telegraph wires to see that they are in a working state. Do you know any thing of that department I mean the mechanical construction of it for he at present is very Ill. However gain what knowledge you can about accounts and writing in general and I hope a Door will be opened for you...Mrs Seward, Henry & Wife, Hadassah & her Partner all unite with me in love to you both and to all the Children...

A final sample of WJ's correspondence is addressed to his young grandson William, aged 5, who, as we shall see, became an engineer and spent a number of years working in India. It was the practice at that time in some schools for older boys to assist with the teaching, as his cousin William Webber is described as doing here. This letter closes with the pious sentiments so frequently in evidence in WJ's correspondence. These sometimes rise to something approaching Biblical eloquence: in an attempt to console William after the death of one of his children, he writes that it is far worse to lose a partner, and expresses the hope that William and Charlotte will survive together 'untill like a full shock of corn you are fit for the Granary of God'. At this point the family were Dissenters, Hadassah for example being christened in the Zion Independent Chapel at East Teignmouth (the Independents are also known as Congregationalists). On 21 January 1856, WJ writes:

> ... my dear Boy I was truly gratified at receiving this first proof of your writing and inditing...Your cousin William Webber [Hadassah's son, who was to become a sculptor: see below] is a Teacher in the School he attends. His Master speaks in the highest terms of him. He wrote an Essay on Drunkenness and smoking which reflected great praise from the audience before whom he delivered it. He wishes to be bound an apprentice to his Master so that he may be capable of taking charge of a School. Your cousin William Seward [Henry's eldest son] goes now to the same School, and I assure you it would be the greatest pleasure I

should enjoy to hear that all my dear Grandchildren were eminent for learning & Piety, except my dear Boy my sincere prayers to God that he may watch over you to keep you from the Paths of Sin & Wickedness by which you are surrounded in London and that as you all grow in years you may grow in the knowledge of our Lord & Saviour Jesus Christ is the earnest prayer of your Grandfather

W J Seward

3. William Rendell Seward (1816 -1884), railwayman

The earliest letter we have from WJ to his son William in London is dated 8 May 1842, sent to him at an address in Stepney. This William may originally have trained as an engraver, but by this time he was working as a Guard on the Dover Railway, and his father is pleased to hear that 'your services are approved by the Company'. By October 1845 William has been offered a post in the East Indies but WJ is strongly against his taking it, on health grounds: 'the Heat of an Eastern climate' would be too much for his wife Charlotte, who is not strong, and with 'Cholera and Fever reigning strong in that part of the world'. Besides, only think if something were to happen to him, leaving a widow with two young children there. At present he is in a good situation with hope of promotion, so should stay. On 11 December 1846, WJ has not heard from him for more than 12 months and is worried about 'what may have happened to you from the nature of your dangerous employment'.

We do not have any correspondence from William himself, but can follow his and his family's progress through his father's letters. In 1838 he had married Charlotte, with whom he had four children. These were born between 1843 and 1850 but were all baptised on the same day, 2 May 1855, at St Mary's

Church, Stratford at Bow. Could this have marked a move from their Dissenting background towards the greater respectability conferred by membership of the Church of England? It must have been a difficult life, with several changes of address and, at one low point in 1846, a Petition of Bankruptcy, in which William is described as 'an Insolvent Debtor' and a 'Trader' – trading in what we do not know.

Illustrated (opposite) are three envelopes among many giving evidence of his frequent moves. Despite such early setbacks he persevered, and was eventually promoted to the prestigious post of Station Master, in around 1860. His brother-in-law William Webber wrote to congratulate him: 'Bless us we shall all be Masters in turn, Monarchs if we live long enough' (he and his father-in-law WJ already being 'Masters' at the Emigrants' Depot).

William has the distinction of being the first Seward of whom we have an image. The fine terracotta bust of him below was sculpted by his nephew William John Seward Webber (1842-1919), son of his sister Hadassah and William Webber (who was himself a wood carver and gilder by training). It is inscribed 'W J S Webber' on the base. He trained in Exeter and at the Royal Academy Schools and frequently exhibited at the RA. After his father's death in 1888 he moved to Harrogate with his mother and practised there until he died, specialising mainly in portrait busts.[24] According to a eulogy in the *Harrogate Advertiser* of 22 March 1919 he was 'a shy unpushful man, careless about money', which inhibited his professional advancement.

To us he may look every inch the respectable Victorian, but William Seward's sister Hadassah was not impressed by the luxuriant beard. On 27 February 1857 she writes to him:

> ...if I had been by the side of you when you said your ugly picture I should have given you a thump on the head for I will not have it to be that there ever was a Seward that was ugly, and the only thing I object to is the Beard. I want to shave that off because you know when last I saw you, you had no beard, but there I like the picture beard and all, I would not spare it again for even so, and Father says the same...

William Rendell Seward

Having achieved success and status as a Station Master, and latterly as an Inspector on the North London Railway, sadly he died following an accident at London's St Pancras Station on 12 September 1884. He was 67. According to a note in the archive, he was taken to University College Hospital after being knocked down and fatally injured by a passing engine. At the subsequent inquest, the cause of death was given as 'fracture of the leg and ribs and other injuries'.

The emigrant's tale:
(Samuel) Henry Rendel Seward (1824 -?)

William's brother Henry's story provides a vivid illustration of the kinds of hardships and adventures encountered by the emigrants once they left Plymouth. His father at one point laments that 'he has the strength of a giant...but he has no head piece'; he had always looked out for him and tried to keep him in work, but after he died in 1858, Henry, whether under pressure from the family or on his own initiative, decided to emigrate to Australia. Born in 1824, he had married at an early age in 1841, and was by this time in his mid-thirties with a wife and several children. These all had to be provided for and taken with him as he travelled around Australia looking for work.

His family connections did at least give them a more comfortable passage than might otherwise have been the case. His uncle William Webber, who was also a supervisor at the depot, writes that he 'spoke to Dr Cumming the Surgeon Superintendent of ship "Escort" he went by, to take him as his assistant a 10£ billet which he granted'.

Samuel Henry Rendel Seward, his wife Elizabeth and one of their children, taken in West Maitland, NSW

Once they arrived in Australia they were on their own. The following long letter to his brother in London describes their wanderings and eventual settlement at West Maitland, New South Wales. It demonstrates his underlying determination and strength of character, and how Australia had given himself and his family opportunities that would never have been available to them in England. After little more than a decade in the country, it is remarkable how well established he and the older children appear to be.

> Sept 30 1872
>
> Devonshire Street
> West Maitland
> N.S.W.
>
> Dear William
>
> It is now 13 years the 11th of this month since we left old England since then we have had many a difficultys and hardships to go throug we have traveled from one country to another the first place where we landed Swan River a very hot country inhabitate chiefly with convicts thinking we could do better in Adelaide so we made our way there we remained at Port Adelaide a fortnight and could get no work there we packed up and started for Adelaide I was there one week. haveing obtain a situation on a station so I traveled one hundred 90 miles up North leaving my Wife and family behind I was there one month on trial so I engage for 12 months I then came back for my Wife and family and when the time exspired I again left for Adelaide so I engage a bullock dray to take all hands back as we used to camp out by night all we had to do was to make our bed under the dray all hands turn in we was as happy there as if we where at home but the worst was the water was so brackish I could not drink it I recollect my going 2 days without a cup of tea and glad I was when we arrive at a place call Hapunda to get a cup of tea then we took train for Adelaide and was there 6 months my eldest son was getting 8/- pr week I never got a stitch of work all the 6 months I was quit disheartened. Seeing an advertisement out for 50 men wanted for Newcastle I was luckily alloted for one we again packed up and was soon on board the steamer we put into Melbourne was there 2 days it is a very large place but I did not see much of it the next place

was Sydney we stopped there to take in the mails then started for Newcastle and was there 3 years I worked on the coal mines all that time Newcastle is a beautiful shipping place surrounded with mines ... was very low and not much work I thought to try my luck on Sydney but there I found there where a great many out of employ and work very scarce so I return back to Maitland where we have lived over 6 years sometimes no work for weeks together I am sure it is quit a task for me to tell you all our trials of hardship with 8 Children to provide for I am thankful to God to think he has led me through it I have 3 Boys 5 Girls the 2 eldest boys are painters by trade William gets 7/6 pr day and has married he has one little boy Samuel gets 5/s pr day he is not very strong but is a young beginner and has always plenty of work till lately which is very scarce I have only one Daughter married she is 300 and 80 miles away from me Mary lives out Alfred the same 3 little ones at home goes to school as for myself I work at anything that comes in my way I have had the good luck of taking Vergers place at St Pauls Church going on 5 years which I get 25 pr year that is very little for the work that is to be done it is better to take that for half a loaf is better than none I am happy to tell you that I have met with a few good friends that will do me a good turn if required I am also happy to tell you that I have got a little more added to my pay for the Church so as to enable me to purchase a nice house of my own it stands in one of the best streets in Maitland and has a nice balconny attach to it there is plenty of room to build another house on the same ground it is a 2 story house in case of floods we can live up stairs without shifting from one place to another as the floods have been very frequently in Maitland one house we lived in the water was over the mantle peace which was very high Maitland is one of the best countrys around New South Wales every kind of fruits, vegetables, maize, lucern, sugar cane, millet and many other thing I cannot think on the mines are very plentiful and many good payable ones they contain tin, copper, gold, silver my eldest Daughter Annes husband has bought 100 and 70 acrs of land at Inverell? 300 and some odd miles from us they have found both copper and tin on it it astonishing to see the number of men that are going away to the diggings day after day some men are getting 2£ pr week and rations some 10£ and rations they have to pay very dear for everything els as things are much dearer than what it used to be meat is much dearer 5d pr pound best joints 4d other salt beef 4d potatoes 8/s pr hd vegetables very scarce butter 1/3? pr pound at the shops but I have not given no more than 10d pr pound all the year round honey 3d eggs 8d this do not come up to the price you have to give in England. Now my Dear Brother I sent you a paper by the last mail I hope you have received it before this comes to your hand I hope these few lines will find you and your family all well I would like for you to keep up correspondence with me in writing as there is no one writes to me now poor Betsey used to write as often as she could but now she is gone its hard to get a letter from any one we are all very well and send love to there Uncle and Aunt and all the Cousins I have sent you the photograph of William he is a voulenteer he has served 5 years and is entitled to 50 acrs of land he has been offered 70£ for it but would not take it because he will be able to get 90 or 100 for it I have not heard anything from Exeter lately I am very glad to hear your daughter is with Lisle they seem so pleased with her. Now I hope you will write me a long letter as soon as you can and give me a plenty of news. Now I must bring this to a close as I am rather late for the mail I have sent a paper with this it is blowing very cold we have had a most fearful dry cold winter with plenty of frost I think I have told you all I can so I conclude with all our best love to Wife and family not forgetting yourself and I remain your affectionate

S.H.Seward

4. William Renell Seward (1845 -?), engineer

William Renell Seward, my great-grandfather, was born and grew up in London. He married Etta (Sarah) Elliott (1852-1938). He appears to have been trained as an engineer, and in 1879 took up a post with the South India Railway. A handwritten extract, dated 15 November 1887, from the Wesleyan Mission Register of Baptisms, Negapatam, District of Tanjore, Presidency of Madras, describes him as 'Engineer to the Forge Foreman'. The extract records the births of my grandfather, William [Thomas] Renell Seward, on 29 October 1880, and his younger brother Ralph Renell on 9 April 1883. Their elder sister

Charlotte Cecilia Hadassah (Lottie) had been born in 1876.

On the voyage out he writes to his parents on 16 June 1879, from 'Ship Australia', that they are all well, with no seasickness, and that 'Baby' is 'the delight of the ship with her never causing problems...[and with] better sealegs than either parent'. Lottie (Tots) was at this time a lively three-year-old. The food is 'first-rate' with fresh meat: live animals are carried, so 'they kill all the meals on board'. His first letter from India, written shortly after the family's arrival in late 1879, describes the later stages of the voyage out, arrival at Madras, and journey across country, followed by his first impressions of the job and living conditions. The first sheet of the letter, pages 1-4, is missing.

> ...women & children all had to go & work in that terrible wilderness [along the Suez Canal?], whether they would or no, no pay, & just sufficient food to keep body & soul together. Thousands died, they are compelled to have dredgers always at work for the sand is continually filling it in. Our next stop was Aden & that's a good deal like Suez. I was glad when we got into the Indian Ocean but there we caught it, but it was cooler, & we saw no more land till Galle was reached in the Island of Ceylon, & there the tropical scenery was superb the tall cocoanut trees the flowers and fruits surpassed anything I ever dreamed of, & we enjoyed our stay.
>
> We were there three days & then left for Madras & landed there at 7 in the morning. Landing is a caution the surf there is so bad even in calm weather that they are obliged to build a certain sort of boat & instead of nailing them together as we do in England they are sewn together with hemp. They are flat-bottomed and as ugly a craft as you could imagine. The ship lay off about 3 miles & you have to do that distance in these craft. They look so fragile & rough made that you expect every moment to see them go to pieces. There are 8 rowers each with a long bamboo and a thing like a saucer attached. The fellow that steers has a like tool, the whole of their garments consist of a bunch of keys that they wear in front so that they feel no inconvenience with their clothes & they have the free use of all their limbs. The ladies trousseau cannot cost a great deal for it consists of a strip of calico 6 in. wide tyed artistically round the loins. Their teeth are the same colour as the ... through chewing the betel nuts. However I am running away from my story of the landing. They waited

till they saw a larger wave than usual then yelling & chattering like a lot of devils they began pulling in & away. We went flying & came on the beach with a thundering bump, that made us think we were going to be rolled onto India head over heels . We stood there a second, then up came another man & picked us up & rolled us up on the beach, broadside on. Like a flash one devil had poor Tots in his arms & scuttled up the beach. Another collared Ett who was already frightened out of her ... and away she went yelling for baby. While this was going on one or two waves came breaking over the boat & threatening to upset the whole bag of tricks me included. Before I could wink I was collared & shouldered & off at full gallop to join my disconsolate mate who had recovered her baby & now began to think of me & then all off to the custom house. Madras is a nice place to land at.

I staid at Madras 3 days, & took train for Cuddalore where we stopt another night. They travel very slow. This is a narrow gauge line & although the stock looks as big as ours the wheels are placed further in under the carriage. We stopt the following night at Tanjore. There I met an old friend of yours named Sam Turner, he has charge of a small loco station there, it being the end of a branch. I was welcomed very kindly all along my route, & although I was only 3 hours from my destination he insisted on my stopping for the night & during the evening we got talking of our, where we sprung from, & directly I mentioned Bow, he knew more about me than I did myself & desires to be remembered to you. Next morn we started for Negapatam & on our arrival was warmly welcomed by the Englishmen there & taken in bathed & feasted. I am now just getting straight in my bungalow & wish you could pop in & crack a bottle with us.

India is not half so bad as tis painted and this place in particular. I am writing this in my verandah. There is very little sun & what there is is shaded by 16 noble great trees all belonging to my compound. I have an acre of ground back & front for garden. The rooms are 25 ft square & so high & look like churches. Bathrooms, stairs with a well[?]all to my own. The cook house is about 150 yards behind. I have not seen a fire since I have been here only in the shop. We only keep 3 servants, the cook, chookra & samacatcher[?] the one like a valet & the other housemaid, & then I send 2 or 3 coolies from the shop to do the rough work. The dobbis, those that do the washing come once a week & take the dirty clothes. We have clean things every day 4 rupees a month. Cotton & linen is very cheap here. Etty bought me some splendid shirts, frilled & worked fronts all hand made 1 rupee each the same would cost 7/6 in London. Everything is cheap except beer & ... is 1/3 ... a leg of mutton weighing 6lb 8 but its dry & hard. I am ... comfortable in my shop. I have 245 men & some of them first rate mechanics, & fine great fellows. They look queer working naked, nothing but a strip of cloth round the loins & no protection at all for the feet in fact they use their toes for tongs & pick up red hot scrap between the big toe & the next & fling it into a box. I am not hard worked either for they are eager to learn & wait on & treat one like a little king, never speak or catch your eye without Salaaming you. I have also ... they are my body servants & interpreters they never leave my side. I have also 4 writers & storekeepers & 2 mastrers[?] that is native foremen who walk about & keep the men at work & convey my orders so I have plenty to help me do nothing & as far as I have got am pretty comfortable.

We have had a lively time with the mosquitoes but have now the curtains up from old. Tots has lost her bloom & begins to look as milky as the rest of them. There is a small fly that infects the eyes, something like the blight in England. She was blind a week with them & now she is smothered with boils, but ginger for pluck, she eats well and rattles about with her boy Joe, whom she orders about in a manner that would delight one on ... of her Aunts. Poor Etty has had very bad eyes & is full of lumps & bumps but is jolly in herself. Thank God, I have escaped as yet excepting a few neat bumps. I wish I could send you a chair like I am sitting in it would fit you properly I will send you a sketch. They are the laziest thing I have seen, you just fall in them, cock a leg on each arm, & enter[?] into the land of dreams. As soon as I can get some Photos done I will send them. In this place we are only 5 minutes walk from the sea. They have a boating club in connection with the works. We could see the water were it not for the trees & the place is smothered with them & they all bloom just like plants scarlet, yellow, white and blue & it has a beautiful effect.

> Well I think I should close this with best love & wishes for yourself, Ma, Renee, Dass, Annie & Harry Lisle & any engineering friends. You might send this letter to Renee & Dass as I shall not be able to write another this mail. Many thanks for the papers you have sent. I have not received a line from any one yet after all their promises. Was very pleased with the Dispatch, Bell. Having a few referees would come kindly & now with best love from Etty & kisses from Tots that God may bless & preserve you all till we meet again is the dearest wish of
>
> Your Affectionate
> Son
> Bill Seward

Etty's letters home at about this time are full of wonder at the place and its people, but bemoan the lack of company and 'amusement'.

> [2 September 1879] ...there's no papers or books of any kind to be got here...Negapatam is considered to be the most healthy station on the line, we have got the sea breeze, I suppose that accounts for it...we will soon be having the cool weather...then we shall be able to go out walking after four in the afternoon...no place to buy furniture we have to get it all made by native carpenters and they are first-rate craftsmen...the servants wear white turbans, white jackets and cloths they are swells...Will wishes me to tell you we have all got Elephantine legs, boils on the end of each of our Probosises as big as strawberries...tell them their papers do come welcome...

> [7 September] I like this place very much indeed, though of course it is very dull, there is no places of amusements of any kind. There is one Protestant church but it is broken and they are forced to hold service on the verandah of his house. [A friend from Will's work and a woman engaged to be married come round in the evenings, making up a four for cards] and we have fine jolly times of it. [There are no horses except those used by Europeans , the natives using bullock carts and 'dandys ...like small omnibus without windows'. Will is going to buy a Phaeton. Another man from Bow has lost his wife so has 'turned against the country'.]

The first photograph of Will is of him in Freemason's attire. He

William Renell Seward, c.1882

had been accepted into the Prudentia Lodge, Number 1859 of Negapatam, on 31 December 1881: the elaborate certificate attesting this survives.

On 20 January 1882 he writes:

> [At Christmas] we were rather quiet & I thought often with a yearning for a seat at the bright fireside and a nice tumbler of Egg Flip. It does not go down here with the same relish even if made as good. [There has been an earthquake. He is trying to arrange a trip to the hills 'to brace us all up'.] We have got the Cholera in the town but the Europeans have not been touched yet, thank god but it makes terrible short work of the natives.
>
> Some of my men have been at work at 9 & buried before 1 midday. My dear Father I send in this a massive gold ring of native workmanship, it is simply pure Gold, and I would like you to put your monogram on the plate and constantly wear it, to bring to your mind that scamp of yours in India. [He and Etta are rearing turkeys, geese and pigeons. Tommy is not yet over his whooping cough and 'Lottie not yet as well as I should like to see her.']

At some point before they left India, at the end of 1887 or early in 1888, a studio photograph was taken of the whole family, the original three now augmented by the two boys born in India: young William (standing) and Ralph.

We do not know exactly when or why they left, but the last stub in Will's Bank of Madras chequebook is dated 17 June 1887, and on 10 November 1887 a certificate was issued from the masonic lodge confirming that he, 'previously to withdrawing from the Lodge satisfied all demands against him'.

We now enter the realms of speculation. It is not clear what happened to Will after this – whether he returned home with his family and continued to work as an engineer, or was incapacitated by sickness until he died. The date of death given on the family tree researched by my brother Tim is 1896, but I have so far seen no corroboration of that. My grandmother Grace Seward thought he died 'about 1890' and there is a photo of him looking older than in the Indian family portrait, taken in London, so probably after his return from India.

My cousin Bridget Harvey-Webb, Lottie's daughter, wrote to my mother in 1988 ('Bill' being my father), 'as you probably know, Bill's father was only about 6 years old when his father died. Will and Ralph, the two boys (Ralph being then about 4) remained with their mother, who lived first in Hove (running an umbrella shop – her agent having absconded) and then in Chelsea, while my mother lived with her cousins the Lisles in Velwell Road [Exeter].' Bridget also supplied the intriguing titbit that Etta, or 'Grannie Seward' as she was later known, 'came from Southsea (where she was shot in the head on the rifle range on the Common as a child, but lived with full faculties to 88)' – or 86 to be precise, if the dates given for her above are correct.

If Will died shortly after leaving India, his elder son William Thomas would have been 7 or 8, which is not too far off Bridget's estimate of 6. Her testimony strongly suggests, therefore, that he did not survive much beyond 1888 or '89.

We next hear of Lottie in 1901, when she was living with her brothers at Upper Mall, Lambeth, and working as a silversmith's assistant, a logical development given her connection to the Lisles, who owned and ran a gold- and silversmith's busiess at 179 Fore Stree, Exeter. In due course she married Hubert

Blanchford, a stained glass artist. Hubert has left us a list of 'Some Churches in which I have been privileged to place Memorial and other windows', the bulk of which are in the West Country (Devon, Cornwall, Dorset and Somerset) but with others appearing in the Home Counties, London, Norfolk, and Kenya (including one in Nairobi Cathedral). I remember her as a very old lady I used to visit at her home in Exeter when I was at Blundell's School in the 1950s. Coincidentally she spent her last year or so in a nursing home about two miles up the road from Blundell's, where I also visited her and where she died in 1963. Having thus known her quite well, but only in old age, it was fascinating to come across this early photograph of her (in the 1920s?) with Grannie Seward.

5 Within Living Memory: The Sewards 1900–1946

Will and Grace 1900 –1928

Both Ralph and William (henceforth 'Will') eventually joined John I. Thornycroft & Co., engineers and shipbuilders, devoting their entire working lives to the firm (of which more later).

The first record of Will subsequent to his birth in India is a card headed '2nd (South Middlesex V.R.)' which notes that he was 'Attested', had a medical examination, and paid his subscription, on 21 March 1898. It marks his joining of the 2nd Battalion of this volunteer regiment, at the age of 17. His address at that time was 42 Upper Mall, Hammersmith (nowadays a most desirable address). A related newspaper clipping about the regimental sports day mentions that Private Seward 'proved the victor, in easy fashion' in the One Mile Bicycle Handicap, with a 20 yards start. There is also a report of an annual inspection of the Volunteers at their HQ, Beaufort House, Fulham, and a circular memorandum of 20 December 1899 calling for 'one Officer and 40 Men of the Corps ...to form part of a Regiment of Volunteer Marksmen, 1,000 strong' who are able 'to leave for South Africa in 15 days.' They must be bachelors aged between 20 and 30, first-class shots, preferably good horsemen, and must enlist 'For the campaign, or for one year...Freedom of the city will be bestowed on each man whose services are accepted.' The call was heeded, as the next item is an invitation to an Impromptu Smoking Concert to be held on 11 January 1900 'as a send off to those members of the Regiment who have enlisted in the City of London Imperial Volunteers and who are about to leave for South Africa.' Will, at 19, would have been too young to join this expedition.

My grandmother Grace Florence (Edwards) Seward was born on 24 September 1885, the birth registered in the parish of Paddington St John, London. A curious survival is the caul (defined as 'a piece of the amniotic sac still attached to a newborn baby's head and face') with which she was born, supposedly a mark of great good fortune, and prized by sailors as a preservative from drowning. The phenomenon is rare, occurring in fewer than in 1 in 80,000 births. It is accompanied by a note from her

Will and Grace Seward

mother: 'Caul of My Only Child Grace Edwards born Sep 24th 1885 at 27, Leinster Terrace, Lancaster Gate, London W'. Her origins are something of a mystery: she never divulged any details at all about her upbringing. Her mother was known as 'Granny Brown' so may have reverted to her maiden name after being widowed. We can infer that Grace had a good basic education, and we know that she spoke without any trace of an accent. She certainly had an enquiring mind and was interested in everything, always determined, through reading and discussion, to be as well-informed as possible.

She and Will were married on 30 June 1906 at Chiswick Parish Church. He was aged 25, she 20, and the occupation of both is given as 'Clerk'. Her father is recorded as Richard Owen Edwards, but both he and Will's father were by this time deceased. The address of both is 'The Laurels, Chiswick Lane', but we need not read too much into this: she may have been living away from her mother by this stage and not wishing to give the address of some temporary lodgings. Perhaps they started their married life renting 'The Laurels'. One has the impression that they could both have been quite lonely at the start of their working lives in London, and that they became very close and reliant on each other. Her grief following his early death at the age of 47 was intense, and she was devoted to his memory for the rest of her long life. The simple words she chose for his monument in Hampton Hill Parish Churchyard were deeply felt: 'An Undying Influence'.

The prominent shipbuilding and engineering company John I. Thornycroft and Co. was founded in 1866, John Isaac Thornycroft having commenced building steam launches at Chiswick in 1864. In 1896 he built his first steam lorry, and the company later became famous for its range of engines, commercial vehicles, ships and fast small craft. It became a public company in 1901 to bring in extra capital. By 1914 its specialities are listed as: marine and mechanical engineering; torpedo craft and launches for river and sea service, propelled by either steam or oil engines; motor boats, motor cars and wagons for heavy transport[25]. Their works were located at Woolston, Southampton (ships and ship repairs); Basingstoke (heavy transport vehicles); and Hampton, Middlesex (small marine craft). Will Seward's and my father Bill's first love was always ships and boats, but Bill worked across all departments of the company in the course of his career. Thornycroft's was highly export-oriented, counting among its customers foreign navies and harbour authorities, as well as the British Admiralty, and purchasers of engines and heavy transport vehicles all over the world. For a farewell lunch marking the retirement of the Hampton yard's manager in 1954, some statistics were prepared. From 1909-1954:

> 604 boats were delivered to various departments of H.M. Government.
>
> 33 countries plus most of the Colonies supplied with Thornycroft boats...
>
> 1919 55ft CMB 41 Knots with 2712 700 b.h.p
>
> 1932 Miss England III 120 m.p.h. Rolls Royce [engine]...

The list ends with a flourish – 'Kings, Princes, Maharajahs etc.'(one of the company's lines was luxury yachts).

Will worked his way steadily up though the Thornycroft's hierarchy, achieving a senior management position by the time of his death. During the First World War he was deeply involved in the production of no fewer than 114 Coastal Motor Boats, his work being recognised by the Admiralty afterwards with the presentation of an imposing silver tankard, fully described in the Prologue to this book. One of these CMBs, with a VC painted on its side, was preserved for many years at the entrance to Thornycroft's yard at Platt's Eyot, Hampton, and duly admired every time we visited 'the Island' to go boating. It is now in the Imperial War Museum, Duxford, with the following label:

> The first twelve 40-foot Coastal Motor Boats (CMBs) were ordered by the Admiralty from J I Thornycroft's in January 1916, and by August were delivered. They were armed with one 18-inch torpedo and Lewis guns, and could make well over 30 knots. CMB 4 was one of this batch. CMB 4

had a most distinguished career. Initially she was based at Dunkirk, operating as part of the Dover Patrol, and taking part in raids on Ostend and Zeebrugge, including the famous Zeebrugge Raid of 23rd April, 1918. In 1919 CMB 4, commanded by Lieutenant Augustus Agar, was used on Secret Service operations in the Baltic. In June Agar and CMB 4 sank the Bolshevik cruiser 'Oleg'. Agar was awarded the VC. In August Agar and CMB 4, with other CMBs participated in Operation RK, the famous attack on Kronstadt Harbour. Two VCs were awarded and Agar received the DSO[26].

A Thornycroft CMB

Will's description of attending the sea trials of a CMB, in a letter of 12 February 1928, bears uncanny similarities to my own experience of attending a Motor Torpedo Boat (MTB) trial in the Thames estuary some 40 years later. Bill had arranged for me to go on this (a great privilege), and I can well remember the thrill of feeling the throb of the powerful engines gathering speed as we raced across the water. The speed attained was comparable, 35 – 40 knots, as far as I can recall. Will writes,

> I went down on the 55 ft. C.M.B. which failed when you were on it. Everybody in connection with the job was blaming the other party for inability to get the speed, & so my function was to squash those tendencies. We got through these preliminary trials very well, doing nearly 38 knots. I shall have to go on the official next week to see the results through. We had a very rough trip which made the results all the better.

On the shipbuilding side, there is a letter of congratulation, dated 19 March 1927, from one K.C. Barnaby (perhaps a director of the firm) 'on the Chilean news, because I do feel that it was primarily due to your efforts'. During the 1920s there appears to have been something of an arms race between Chile and Argentina, with British shipbuilders vying with each other to supply both countries, under the auspices of the Admiralty. Thornycroft's was bidding to supply destroyers to the Chilean navy. Barnaby continues: 'Time and again we have got out better designs than our competitors – or think we have – only to see them get the order through more skilful handling of the Admiralty officials.' On this occasion, Thornycroft's had been successful, the implication being that the favourable outcome was due to Will's 'skilful handling'.

The personal cost of these 'efforts' is feelingly brought out in a letter of 30 March 1927 from Will to my father at his boarding school, expressing bitter disappointment at being unable 'to attend one of the most important events of your life' – the boy's Confirmation.

> ...I am deep in the throes of a most trying & difficult series of negotiations on the success of which may depend work for over 2000 and possibly 3000 men for 2 years...Having been told we have the contract is by no means the end of the work. It is only the beginning!...I must close now as I have a huge contract to read through. What a life!

His hard work and success brought compensations. As well as being able to afford to send his children to good private schools (Malvern College for Dorothy, the elder, and Blundell's for Bill) and to rent a substantial house in Teddington, the family had a boat. The letter continues, 'I've named our sailing boat "EIDOTHEA" which if you know your Odyssey you will see is quite a good name.' (Eidothea was a sea nymph, daughter of Proteus, who saved Menelaus and his crew from starving to death and showed them the way from Egypt to their home.)

The Hampton yard also took on non-naval work, including luxury yachts. A 'River Boat Yacht for the King of Egypt', from 1927, could possibly have been the craft pictured at its launch overleaf.

Bill and his father both loved engines – an enthusiasm my brother Tim and I were, alas, unable to share, although Jeremy was more in tune with it. (We must have been a sore disappointment to Bill in this respect.) The following extract amusingly illustrates their shared interest:

> As regards the sample of material you took out of the gear case, I'm afraid I was not able to judge very well, though I cannot admire its taste. You see I was reading your letter

Launch of a yacht at the Hampton yard: Will Seward far left of the group on the platform

> over my dressing table on which I had a breakfast cup of egg-in-tea, & was still looking for the rag while finishing the cup, when I found it in my mouth!! It dropped off the letter into the cup! Anyway the filings or bright material which still adhered to the rag is only what one would expect, and it is to remove this possible risk of damage to bearings that the oil has to be changed so early.

Grace always said what fun Will was, and these few letters amply demonstrate his warmth and humour.

His last letter to Bill is dated 12 February 1928. It is a lengthy discussion of the 15-year-old's mock exam results, which subjects he should concentrate on, whether he needs extra tuition, and what qualifications he should go for in future. Cambridge is mentioned, and the arguments for and against a 'Varsity' training, as against immediate practical experience, are rehearsed. He also gives sensible advice on exam technique. It ends with the description of the CMB trials quoted above, and encloses a copy of Bill's school report for the term ending in December 1927. Unfortunately the report is not a good one, and the terse comment 'VERB.SAP.' ('a word to the wise') is added at the foot. Although there is no indication at this point that he had any inkling of what was about to happen, it is remarkable that this letter reads as such a conscious effort to map out his son's future – almost as a final testament.

His death, from 'duodenal ulceration and acute heart failure'

On a family holiday, 5 July 1926: Will and Dorothy. The car is an Armstrong-Siddeley.

was only three weeks away, on 1 March 1928. The certificate describes him as 'Sales Manager (Engineer)'. He died at the Empire Nursing Home, Vincent Square, following an operation, presumably for the ulcer. According to Grace, he was well aware that the procedure was extremely risky, but he planned for a successful outcome: a pencilled draft note to the Station Master at Teddington, three days before his death, requests that the unused portion of his season ticket should be credited to the next ticket. This suggests that the operation was about to take place, and that he survived for a day or two after it, before the heart attack which killed him.

Bill, in Devon, knew nothing of the disaster as it unfolded in London, but rushed home for the funeral and returned to Blundell's a day or so later. His letters home to Dorothy and Grace immediately after the event are remarkably calm, and he is clearly doing all he can to keep up their spirits. Only in his second letter from Blundell's, dated 9 March, does he reflect on their loss, referring specifically to the letters quoted above: 'it is simply marvellous how everything [Daddy] said then applies equally well now and I should think will always apply.' Perhaps it was for this reason that these particular letters were kept. There is a very clear sense that Will's example will continue to direct their actions: 'you know what he wanted us to do and I am sure that with other people's kindness we shall be able to do it quite comfortably.' It is God's will and for the best. Sadness creeps in only in the small details: 'We must look after the pond properly because Daddy built it and loved it.'

Writing about this period is rendered yet more poignant with the knowledge of hindsight. Will's death at the age of 47 (like *his* father, who appears to have died in his forties) was the first of three such devastating blows over the ensuing decades. Bill was to die at 53, and his second son Tim at 51: four successive generations of children deprived of their fathers in youth or early adulthood. The causes of death varied, so cannot be genetic, but it is a hard dispensation that the family has had to bear. It is idle to speculate on the long-term effects of such losses, but beyond doubt life is the poorer for them, whatever other compensations may come our way. When life is going well, we wish our fathers could have been there to share our good fortune; when badly, we miss their wisdom, love and support.

Grace, Dorothy and Bill 1928–1939

On the surface, life continued as before. As early as 17 March, a letter arrived informing Grace that the Thornycroft Benevolent Fund would be forwarding to her a cheque for £1000, 'and also, for the purpose of educating and training your son and daughter, £100 per quarter will be paid over to you for the next two years, starting from 1 April 1928.' It was understood that Bill would be taken on as a pupil at the end of this period, 'at any of the Works you select', with the company undertaking to provide an as yet unspecified contribution to expenses during his training.

So Bill's future course was clear. He returned to school and, in the same year as his father's death, underwent the ordeal of taking the School Certificate exam in July, gaining credits in five subjects, and, in December, London Matriculation, in five subjects. Thereafter, until he left Blundell's in April 1930, he does not appear to have been working towards any further exams. In the family's straitened circumstances Cambridge was no longer an option, so he concentrated instead on gaining all he could from the extracurricular opportunities the school had to offer.

He enjoyed the sport, attaining his 2nd XV colours and some success in athletics, as a sprinter. He seems to have found a kindly father figure in the Westlake housemaster, G.V. Hotblack, and developed a lifelong friendship with Charles Moore, who had lost both his parents and was also destined to become an engineer (civil in his case). Bill ended his time at Blundell's as Head of House and a School Monitor: a responsible, thoughtful and conventionally religious young man. His longest surviving letter from this time is a description of his attendance, as one of the banner-bearers representing the school, at a Toc H ceremony in London: Toc H, founded by 'Tubby' Clayton during the war as an 'Everyman's Club' for soldiers in the trenches, was an interdenominational association for Christian social service. But there was much fun and laughter as well, with an especially vivid description of everyone having a wonderful time skating and tobogganing after a heavy snowfall in February 1929. In the background, too, were Aunt Lottie and Uncle Hubert and his cousins in Exton, just south of Exeter, where he was always welcome.

His last letters from Blundell's are full of optimism and plans for the future. On 27 February 1930, thinking of the approaching anniversary of Will's death, he writes:

> Through your colossal bravery and work we, Dorothy and I, are now pretty nearly living the same life with the same wonderful example to follow, as if Daddy had been here... I often wonder whether for you the prospect is still rather uncertain. For me I'm sure it is not. If everything follows the ordinary rule of Life Dorothy should soon be married and I should be earning a moderate income so that for you, your life's work is done and you have but to sit back and enjoy it, so to speak.

Dorothy (always known as 'Boo') by this stage had graduated from London University and was earning a living in journalism, working as a reporter for *The Surrey Comet*. Grace was taking in lodgers, many of them foreign. His very last letter from the school, on 4 April, continues the cheerfully upbeat note:

> I'm so glad to think that you have the same ideas as I have about a family life. At present, to be the father of a fine family is my greatest ambition. I often think of it and often think of ours: if I can do the same as Daddy and you have, for any sons of mine then I shall really feel that I have not failed in my life's work and purpose. At present I regard my career and the importance of it as a necessary adjunct to the attainment of a good home life.

Home was Cromer House, Hampton Road, Teddington, a substantial Victorian dwelling with a large garden and tennis court. When the family was about to leave it in late 1931, Grace mentions that she will have to negotiate the date with 'the Office of Works' which suggests that she and Will had rented it from the government. Some years later, in March 1945, it was taken over by the nearby National Physical Laboratory. Alan Turing, following his wartime work on Enigma at Bletchley Park, was based there from 1 October 1945, when he took up a post in the newly

Front entrance to Cromer House

A tennis party c.1930. Grace third from left, seated. Bill at front wearing his Blundell's blazer.

Below: Garden and rear of Cromer House.

established Mathematical Division of the NPL. He had a small room in the north wing, where he worked on his 'Automatic Computing Engine': the rest, as they say, is history[27]. (Reg Debnam, my brother Tim's father-in-law, who worked at the NPL, remembered the house well.)

Bill joined Thornycroft's straight from school as a 'premium pupil', starting his training at the Woolston works near Southampton. He continued to stay in contact with Hotblack and another master at the school, W.R. Lewin, who writes about their shared enthusiasm for sailing and cars, school matters, and the regret of all that he could not have 'stayed to be Head of the School next term: we want a good one to help our new Headmaster and give him a good impression.' There is talk of his joining Toc H, taking a TA commission and joining a rowing club, but uncle Ralph Seward, writing as a seasoned Thornycroft's man from Rio de Janeiro, warns against taking on too much, with the new academic year looming in the autumn. Ralph's son, Howard, had already started his training at the Basingstoke works.

Three very full years of work experience and exams lay ahead. Afterwards, Bill broke it down as follows: 2 years 3 months at Woolston, with 1 to 10 months in each department; 8¼ months at Basingstoke, with much shorter periods in each section; attending trials at Plymouth; all in tandem with working towards the Institution of Mechanical Engineers qualification at University College, Southampton. This is all concisely summarised in a CV he drafted in later life:

> Training in Marine Engineering at Company's Southampton Shipyard. Practical experience from Pattern Shop through to fitting on board and trials of a variety of turbine and reciprocating and auxiliary machinery also water tube boilers for ships up to 5000 tons including destroyers: liner repairs in Southampton Docks: engine Drawing Office.
>
> Training in heavy motor vehicle engineering at Company's Basingstoke Works. Automotive type diesels and gearboxes – heavy chassis components – assembly and testing practical work – Drawing office.
>
> Institution of Mechanical Engineers examination sections 'B' and 'C'. [He became an Associate Member in 1939.]

Section 'B' was mainly technical, including Properties and Strength of Materials, and Steam and the Steam Engine; Section 'B' was more concerned with Economics and Management.

He lived in a succession of 'digs' as he moved around, acquired a motorbike, and mixed with various other young men at the start of their careers, including 'one fellow who was a Communist but has since cooled off a bit and now reads Economics really seriously. He has a most amazing memory and seems to understand it all.' He greatly enjoyed the trips to Plymouth, where he was able to go for long tramps on the moors, do some sailing, and drink plenty of 'Cyder' on high days and holidays. The town still retained an old world charm, with cobbled streets and noisy fishmarket, but also with a fine new swimming pool carved out of the cliffs, and the Hoe beautifully kept and illuminated at night. Much of this ambience was irretrievably lost a few years later when Plymouth was so badly hit by the air raids: I remember it in the 50s as a rather sad, bleak place.

Bill's 21st birthday, 25 April 1933, chimed neatly with the end of his pupillage, and generated a clutch of congratulatory letters from older family members. One was from his Grandma (Etta) Seward, a very old lady living in Exeter, long returned from India and widowed many years before. Amidst the conventional good wishes for a bright future, a remark from Aunt Lottie stands out:

> I have not the slightest doubt for you, my dear, as you are all that your Father would have wished, and I am sure you will go ahead just as he did only you have the advantage of not having to fight as he did which gives you a start.

With mounting difficulties in the industry and the massive interruption of the war, life was never to be that easy, but the comment was in other respects a fair one.

From 1933 to 1939 Bill was Technical Sales Representative for heavy motor vehicles, working from Head Office in Smith Square, Westminster. It is not clear why, through these years, he was not given the opportunity of working on the marine side, which he would almost certainly have preferred, but perhaps there were no vacancies. The job entailed attendance at regular trade shows, a pattern which continued throughout his career, latterly the high point of the year being the annual Boat Show at Olympia. A touch of light relief is provided by a letter of 7 November 1933 from his current girlfriend Leila Hosking:

> I suppose now that you are up on the Stand at Olympia you are the true Showman, washing your hands with invisible soap, all bland and suave!! I think I'll have to come and see for myself. What will you sell me, a lorry or a steam engine?

Grace had left Cromer House in the autumn of 1931 and taken a flat or small house at 11c, The Crescent, Surbiton. This enabled her, much to her relief, to give up taking in lodgers, referred to with some irritation in the family correspondence as 'the Foreign Bods' or simply 'F.B.s'. Dorothy would have been based here while she worked at the *Comet*, and Bill after he completed his training. The two of them would often partner each other at dances. At about this time, Grace was able to take a Mediterranean cruise with a friend (possibly to celebrate liberation from the F.B.s?) to the Peloponnese and Sicily, calling at Nafplion and Palermo.

Our sources then lead us to early 1939, with hints of preparation for the looming conflict. On 25 April he writes from Tallinn, having embarked on the cargo ship *Baltavia* on a passage through the Kiel Canal into the Baltic, gaining experience in the solution of navigational problems. By this time he was almost certainly training with the Naval Reserve. The captain advised that 'it would be better to give rise to no questions from the German pilot, "And anyway", says he, "why the hell should they know what we're doing in England"'(very *Riddle of the Sands*!). One fellow-passenger was 'an RAF fellow who has been sent to Esthonia [*sic*] for 9 months to learn Russian'. He admires the quiet competence of the Estonian crew and looks forward to seeing the consul in Tallinn, 'some of my business people', and exploring the city. On the 30th he was halfway back across the North Sea, expecting to arrive in Hull about midnight. The purpose of the trip was to brush up his navigation skills for a naval exam, and to experience working alongside the officers, trying his hand at steering the ship, while at the same time using the opportunity to explore potential business contacts in the region.

By September he had been called up and was comfortably billeted at the Palace Hotel, Southend-on-Sea, enjoying 'first-class fare and conditions'. Boo had just got married to Bob Kidd, a prosperous Birmingham businessman; and Grace was on ARP duty. He is expecting to be made a sub-lieutenant soon and is to be measured for his uniform at Austin Reed's. The job at Southend is to board 'the merchant ships lying off in the river, so as to collect details for arranging convoys...There is most of the London RNVSR [Royal Naval Volunteer Supplementary Reserve] crowd here and things certainly look too cushy!' At this stage of the phoney war there was not a great deal to do, with plenty of time for the officers to get in a bit of sailing and for drives out into the countryside, but by early January he is expecting an imminent change of job. However, he feels it would be wise not to make too much fuss about it or he might end up with something worse, like 'balloon barrages'. He hopes his mother can negotiate a reduction in rent since neither he nor Dorothy, who had contributed around half, are now living there, and advises her to 'park the car with someone for the duration'.

The next we hear of him by letter he is based in Belfast, on real convoy duty.

Love, war and marriage 1939-1942

Bill's wartime letters to Maureen form a complete series, most marked by him as 'On Active Service'. These have either a printed label 'EXAMINER [plus number]' pasted vertically along the left-hand side of the envelope, or are rubber stamped 'From H.M. Ship. Passed by Censor', with a space for his initials, and the date, to be written in. Occasionally, tiny pieces of text have been scissored out by the censor.

After an initial course at *HMS Wildfire*, a training establishment at Sheerness, and six months serving on *Ullswater*, a minesweeping trawler, he had been given command of his first ship on 1 October 1940[28]. This was the 'Dance' Class anti-submarine trawler *Saltarelo*, on convoy duty from Belfast. The routes taken by the convoys were of course highly secret at the time but

Sub-Lieutenant Bill Seward

we know that a good deal of the work was around the Scottish coast and into the North Sea, with forays into the North Atlantic on the Canadian run. Some convoy escorts would meet eastbound ships in mid-Atlantic and then shepherd them back to British waters: this was particularly dangerous as Canadian and British air cover could not reach that far. The codes of the convoys, with dates and routes, are now listed on a website from which links may be made to individual ships[29], so it is possible to plot the routes taken by Bill's. For example, on 12 June 1944 his 'Flower' class corvette *Loosestrife* joined convoy ETM 007, Thames to France, returning with the convoy the next day: this was part of the operations following D Day on 6 June.

Maureen, as we have seen, was 'canteening' at this stage, in the officers' mess on Belfast docks. Did their eyes meet as she proffered him an especially generous portion of steak and kidney pudding (he was always hungry)? At any rate, by 8 January 1941 they were 'an item', possibly already engaged, judging by the pranks played on him by his shipmates – such as an onion wrapped in his pillowcase and labelled 'Sweet dreams'. Other letters paint a picture of a happy man on a happy ship, enjoying the company of his messmates, playing classical gramophone records in quiet moments, but missing her and jealous of the dances and social life she was still enjoying ashore.

Here is a sample of his general mood and of how life on shipboard was for him.

> H.M.S. Saltarelo
> 21 November 1941
>
> ....Anyhow I do hope you have a grand time. The last two occasions at the Base have seemed, so far as I was concerned, such a rush and a tear, and for the first few days anyhow, I have I suppose been too tired to want to do anything but enjoy the warmth and quiet of Belhaven. But it is no use getting into a stodge and it is fun to go to a few dances etc so I hope we can manage it. And although, (without shooting a line in any way!) life at sea is getting distinctly stiffer now with the long darkness and gales, a change and a spot of 'the light fantastic' at the Base is probably every bit as much of a rest as 'sittin' around the

fire at home. But you'll have to 'ginger me up' please or else you'll find me just 'sittin' again – and that's no fun for you anyhow – you can do that all the time I'm away.

Officers' quarters

The weather just now is foul, with squalls and a gale. Luckily, however, it is astern of us for a while until we round the next corner when we shall just start rolling like merry hell as we did the night before last. I hate this not only because it makes almost everything on board impossible but also it always makes my blinking thigh start aching again...whatever it is, it depresses me to have an ache in my leg whenever it's rough and also to have a weak limb to get about on.

I'm missing Hindson's cheery bright efficiency this trip, as although the relief officer is very reliable and good as far as he goes, he cannot replace No.1. and further he is of a very quiet serious disposition – not the best of company in a Wardroom.

Have got one particularly nice tweed sample for your coat – and two others not so hot. Have also earmarked my Lovatt tweed, sent Mother her length – and sent more shortbread to your Mother. Had quite a busy morning there. Couldn't get your Mother's woollen scarf as they must have two coupons. Such a pity. Especially as it does not look as if we shall go to any other shopping centre this side.

wwwwwwWWWWWOW!! that was a near one. I heard the most horrible selection of helm and engine-room- telegraph orders coming down the bridge voicepipe and after standing it as long as I could I went rushing up to find the ship virtually turning circles round itself in the middle of the convoy with ships on all sides – all this at 10 o'c at night in pitch

On the bridge

> dark and rain – and the officer of the watch saying 'By now I don't know which way I'm going!' Very unnerving I assure you – especially as in our present guise we are nearly invisible at night. Phewwwwww.....
>
> *Sunday 23rd*
>
> Well, this has been just one hell of a trip as far as weather is concerned and last night was not pleasant including as it did a complete scattering of our sheep necessitating rounding-up in the dark. In the middle of it all our steering jambed and put us into a bit of a fix. However, all is now well – Gould and I are in my cabin listening to the Sunday afternoon concert and the weather has fined away completely. For the last 24 hours until noon today I have had a limp 'body' on my settee – one of the seamen who was laid out completely with sea-sickness – I had him dumped here because the motion is rather less amidships than forward.
>
> This morning we had quite fun sinking a floating mine by rifles. I'm afraid we are all rather out of practice on such bobbing targets though....
>
> I'll be back just as soon as the 'Saltcellar' can bring me. – Cheeribye!

His last addressed to 'Miss Maureen Clarendon' was dated 24 January 1942, in which he hopes she enjoys a trip to Dublin with 'lots of lights everywhere and no carping for coupons etc.' They were married on Wednesday 4 March 1942 at Drumbo Parish Church, Ballylesson, Co. Down.

'Dance' Class trawler T128, HMS Saltarelo

A tale of three ships: *Saltarelo, Loosestrife,* and *Inver*

Bill commanded three ships during World War II. The first, as we have seen, was *HMS Saltarelo*, of which he took command as a sub-lieutenant on 1 October 1940. These 'Dance' class armed trawlers were designed for anti-submarine and minesweeping work. They had a displacement of 545 tons, with a length of 164 feet and beam (width) of 27 ft. 8 in., speed 12 knots; as armament they carried one 4 in. gun, three anti-aircraft guns, and 30 depth charges. The crew consisted of 40 men. *Saltarelo* was built by Henry Robb, Ltd, Leith, and launched in August 1940.

The class was celebrated by *Punch* in a poem entitled 'Dancing to War', by 'Fo'c'stle', published on 13 August 1942[30].

> If I would picture in a single frame
> The dual essence of the small ships' war
> I'd choose the 'Dance' Class trawlers for my theme:
> Short, shallow-drafted, funnel and fo'c'stle low,
> With depth charge towers and a 4 in. gun,
> Flaunting White Ensigns four abreast in port,
> Rolling like sea-cows in a Northern gale,
> Gay in their dazzle paint -
> Grey, blue, green and white
> Happy and hard, dangerous and bright...

The rest of the poem evokes the hard life and comradeship aboard and ends by playing with the romantic names of the ships:

> Dancing grim as a fencer is grim
> *Tango, Morris Dancer* and *Minuet*
> *Saltarelo* and *Sarabande*
> As the sword in the fencer's hand...

In truth, much of the work could be tedious, as well as hard in bad weather. At one point he writes, 'All I hope is we get a chance to do our stuff this time. If ever I was in the mood to "have a crack" it is just now and it would be grand to have the chance to do a bit more than just "sheep-dogging" of the stragglers and generally acting as nursemaid to the merchantmen.' His last letter on *Saltarelo* notepaper is dated 26 October 1942, but his command of her had officially ended on 1 October.

On 12 September 1940 he had been promoted to Lieutenant, but after *Saltarelo* there followed what must have been a frustrating period of two and a half years, during which he moved around the country, from posts in Scotland to the base at Portland, engaged in training and other activities. He was not given another ship until July 1944. To set against this, a great deal was happening in his personal life, and at least he was not on dangerous and exhausting convoy duty when he married, and when Maureen gave birth to their first child (the present author) on 8 September 1943. It would be wearisome to attempt to trace all his movements at this time. Briefly, they honeymooned (or 'funnymooned' as they joked, it being in the peculiar circumstances of wartime) at the Allan Water Hotel, Bridge of Allan, Stirlingshire, and later took a flat in Colinton Road, Edinburgh, so that she could be near him while he was based in Leith.

After Tony's birth, Maureen and the baby stayed in the parental home at 'Belhaven', which once again became a beacon of peace and comfort, now for a young family. Although Bill was not there at the time of the birth, whenever he was on leave he could hasten over to Belfast to see them and to rest and recover. Maureen and Tony were looked after with the greatest care and love by her parents and the maid and other helpers, and Bill had a comfortable and welcoming home to return to whenever his duties allowed.

The next major development was the build-up to D-Day on 6 June 1944. Bill is spending a good deal of time with American fellow-officers and eating better than usual, courtesy of the 'American Messes'. He is based in Methil, Fife, and clearly something big is about to happen. On 25 May he writes to his father-in-law Victor Clarendon ('Pop') enclosing a letter to be passed to Maureen should anything happen to him in the coming days. It details all the 'business' matters to be seen to in case of his death, and who is to receive certain precious mementoes. Its conclusion must echo the feelings of so many in wartime faced with the imminent possibility of extinction, but is at the same time a unique and eloquent expression of his own personality.

> I hope this letter will not strike you as odd but I want you to know that if this is to be my last Navy job, the importance of it and the part I think I can play in it are such that I am now fully resigned to it as a necessary aid to the general betterment we all aim for. I am not frightened about what may happen to me but I am desperately sad at the interruption it will cause in our being together and the stop it will put to our mutual plans. I am also sad to think that such distress must come to you and that it will throw extra responsibilities on you as far as Tony is concerned and I hate to think of you lonely. But with all this I also know that you have just the very qualities and loveliness of nature to overcome these things and make a grand job of it all. That my dear is a wonderful knowledge for me to have at these times and the greatest help any man could have short of your actually being with me. Coupled with my memories of you, with the knowledge of Tony being in such good hands, I have indeed that mental satisfaction and happiness which is the strongest fortification in difficult times.
>
> If I have to go on 'somewhere else' my main excitement – yes it amounts to that – is to find out if in fact I am to lose all touch with you and Tony or whether in fact we pick up the threads again at some time or other. The latter is a most thrilling and lovely prospect my dearest wife.

Fortunately all went well for him, and on 17 June he writes to his mother from 'Belhaven', 'I am sitting in the garden indulging in the age-old pastime of adoring my own child!'. We now know that his task on D-Day was to sail a redundant American ship to a position close to the Arromanches beaches and sink it, as a block-ship. The block-ships were laid to protect the waters off the beaches in bad weather, providing a shelter for the coasters and other small craft performing a shuttle service between ship and shore. The extent of this service was enormous, employing between 2,000 and 3,000 craft and about 15,000 men. According to a newspaper report[31] the assembling of these ships, not required for other purposes, resulted in a very motley fleet capable of only the slowest speed – a cause of great anxiety when D-Day had to be postponed for 24 hours due to violent storms. The Americans had not been able to remove the equipment on board, so the skeleton crew came away with all they could carry. Bill managed to secure blankets and a bivouac tent with 'U.S.' stencilled on it, which saw much use in our childhood.

He was given command of his second ship, *Loosestrife*, on 3 July 1944, relinquishing it on 13 January 1945. According to the record referred to above, she took part in 26 convoys during this time. These were mostly in support of the invasion, from Thames to France and back, but with three longer forays: Liverpool to New York; Halifax, Nova Scotia to UK; and Methil to Bergen. Many years later, on a business trip to Halifax, I was thrilled to discover in the harbour the only remaining 'Flower' Class corvette still in existence, the Canadian Navy ship *Sackville*, now a floating museum. Visitors can explore every part of it, from stem to stern, and I couldn't help being struck by how small it was and how very cramped the quarters must have been: this was a vessel carrying a crew of 90 men. 'Flowers' were nearly twice the tonnage of Dance Class trawlers, and 208 feet in length as against 164 feet, but still small for the demands placed upon them by Atlantic conditions. *Loosestrife* was built by Hall, Russell and Co. in Aberdeen and launched in 1941.

'Flower' Class corvette *HMS Loosestrife K105*

The hardships of serving in corvettes are evoked in Nicholas Monsarrat's memoir *Three Corvettes* and his bestselling novel *The Cruel Sea*, the latter made into a hugely popular film after the war[32]. The following extract from Wikipedia, drawing on several sources, gives a vivid impression of what the crews had to endure.

> Service on Flowers in the North Atlantic was typically cold, wet, monotonous and uncomfortable. Every dip of the forecastle into an oncoming wave was followed by a cascade of water into the well deck amidships. Men at

action stations were drenched with spray, and water entered living spaces through hatches opened to access ammunition magazines. Interior decks were constantly wet and condensation dripped from the overheads. The head (or sanitary toilet) was drained by a straight pipe to the ocean; and a reverse flow of the icy North Atlantic would cleanse the backside of those using it during rough weather. By 1941 corvettes carried twice as many crewmen as anticipated in the original design. Men slept on lockers or tabletops or in any dark place that offered a little warmth. The inability to store perishable food meant a reliance on preserved food such as corned-beef and powdered potato for all meals.

The Flowers were nicknamed 'the pekingese of the ocean'. They had a reputation of having poor sea-handling characteristics, most often rolling in heavy seas, with 80-degree rolls, 40 degrees each side of upright, being fairly common; it was said they 'would roll on wet grass'. Many crewmen suffered severe motion sickness for a few weeks until they acclimatised to shipboard life. Although poor in their sea-handling characteristics, the Flowers were extremely seaworthy; no Allied sailor was ever lost overboard from a Flower during World War II, outside combat.

A typical action by a Flower encountering a surfaced U-boat during convoy escort duties was to run directly at the submarine, forcing it to dive and thus limiting its speed and manoeuvrability. The corvette would then keep the submarine down and pre-occupied with avoiding depth charge attacks long enough to allow the convoy to pass safely. The 16-knot (30 km/h) top speed of the Flower-class ships made effective pursuit of a surfaced U-boat (about 17 knots) impossible, though it was adequate to manoeuvre around submerged U-boats or convoys, both of which ran at a typical maximum of 8 knots, and sometimes much less in poor weather. The low speed also made it difficult for Flowers to catch up with the convoy after action[33].

Bill's last and grandest ship was *Inver*, a 'River' Class frigate, number K302, which he commanded from 3 February 1945 to early in 1946. A few months earlier, in October 1944, he had been promoted to Lieutenant Commander, the rank he held until demobilisation in April 1946. With a length of 283 feet and top speed of 20 knots, the 'River' frigates' range was double that of the corvettes, up to 7,200 nautical miles at 12 knots; under his command were 7 officers and 120 men. A fine framed watercolour of *Inver*, by Leslie Carr, has a detailed inscription on the back written by Bill.

> Frigate 1500 tons built Canada 1942
>
> WRS in command 1945/6
>
> **English Channel** troop convoys for the liberation of Europe
>
> **Scotland & N. Ireland** Anti-U-boat (Schnorkel) patrols
>
> **East Indies Escort Force** based Ceylon- Singapore – Malacca Straits- Sabang – Madras
>
> – out & return via Mediterranean and Suez Canal
>
> Returned USA early 1946 under Lease-lend

The recent German development of the 'schnorkel' (literally 'nose') enabled U-boats to stay under water for far longer than previously, drawing in air through a tube and observing the surface through a periscope. It rendered them almost impossible to locate and, for a while, cancelled out Allied superiority in radar. The Allied countermeasures involved the setting up of support groups of anti-submarine vessels that were sent out over wide areas, beyond the immediate vicinity of the convoys, to hunt down U-boats before they could attack[34].

Life on board was fairly relaxed, with no immediate threats in the offing. We still have a silver-plated 'Inter-Watch Competition' cup presented by the Preston, Ontario chapter of the Imperial Daughters of the Empire, who had 'adopted' the ship. These ladies busied themselves with sending various comforts to the crew, and their representative, Mrs A.P. Sharpe, became a lifelong friend of Bill's. I am not sure that they ever

'River' Class frigate *HMS Inver K302*

met, but she continued to send small gifts to the family for many years after the war.

For Bill as commanding officer, the welfare of the men was a major concern. The following is an example of the kind of problem he had to deal with in what we would nowadays call his 'pastoral' capacity.

[*to his mother*] 28 June 1945

> ....One other letter I've had is from the wife of one of our ratings who has been having difficulty at home and with whom I've had many discussions – given special leave etc. His wife who must be in the early 20s has one youngster, another coming in Sept. and keeps house for her father-in-law who is almost blind and very irritable. I have been trying unsuccessfully to get a compassionate draft for him so that he can pop home every two or three weeks to keep the peace between his old father and stop him being unreasonable to the wife. From her letters to me (this is the second) she must be a very sweet girl and the position at the moment is that she is fixed up for a hospital in September, the first kiddy is fixed up in a home for the time in question and the Blind Association and Army Welfare are arranging for help to come to the house for the old man while the daughter-in-law is away. Welfare are providing the help and Blind Ass. paying for it. (My lad is just an able seaman) The real question now I think is help in the house when the daughter-in-law gets back with her second kiddy i.e. 14 days after it arrives. This family whose name is HEFFERNAN live at
>
> 41. TRINITY ALMSHOUSES
MILE END ROAD
MILE END E.1.
>
> And I wondered if it came within Mrs. Brunskill's area – and if so whether she could do anything to help find assistance in the house for the time afterwards – a few weeks at least. We can arrange money from the ship if necessary. Would you let me know and I will write her or perhaps there is enough above to deal with it.

Bill's final letter from *Inver* is headed 'Port Said 27 Dec.', en route to home. Earlier he had written to say that he expected to dock at Portsmouth on 10 January, and hoped Maureen might be able to hire a car and meet him there. We must assume that he handed the ship over soon after his return early in 1946, and was in due course demobbed. He had been on active service for nearly 6½ years, from September 1939 until long after the end of the war in Europe (VE Day, 8 May 1945).

One can only imagine the frustration of all those who were sent out to the Far East to finish the war there, only to find that by the time they arrived it was all over. On 24 April he had written 'all the navy will go East when Germany is finally out – and Inver with them' – which she duly did, setting off from the UK in late July. This extract is from a letter to his mother of 13 August 1945, the day before VJ Day when Japan surrendered, finally bringing the war to a close. He is in Colombo, Ceylon, after 'three weeks' hard steaming' from the UK, via the Suez Canal.

> ....No, we didn't go through the Straits, nor did the other spot appeal to me one little bit – we used it in daylight and to me it was simply dreadfully hot and pitifully slow entailing being on the bridge from 0700 till 1830 though certainly with nothing to do except make sure the Pilot didn't suddenly go 'berserk'. I'm awfully glad to have seen it all and above all to have heard the remarks from the poor Tommies stuck out in the desert who were bathing as we passed and greeted us with 'You're too late chum. It's ruddy well finished' or 'Whatcher goin' that way for'. Poor fellows it must be an awful life in the desert, especially with the war thousands of miles away.

However, the posting certainly had its compensations, not least the time to write long letters home describing his experiences in this exotic region. The following, to Maureen, are generally in euphoric mood, bringing Bill's wartime experience to a triumphant close.

Sept 7th 1945

> ...life is very comfortable with good weather, calm sea and a nice jog-trot job which will get much more interesting in the next few days as we reach our destination in the Malacca Straits (isn't it fun to give place names). From there we don't know where we go tho' I guess we shall see Singapore before very much longer and even Hong Kong maybe. Incidentally coming out our stops were Gibraltar, Port Said (where the bathing was so good) and then straight to Colombo. The big procession was at Kandy

(what a fine spilling of the beans!)

Another good thing is that the Radio is coming alive again. Round some of the parts we have been reception is very bad. Much of what we can get is Tamil or Indian music which is most queer and catlike but we can get regular news bulletins and in the evening some music relayed from home. They are using India Ceylon and Singapore Broadcasting stations for many official announcements both to our own forces and the Japanese – giving the latter their orders for surrender, where, how, when etc. All very historic and interesting. Also heard the Singapore Station when it first started up after the occupation. Very interesting and an excellent quick bit of work by someone. There was a most moving half an hour on Singapore radio last night when two people who had been interned throughout the occupation spoke and the Bishop of Singapore who has also been interned thro'out conducted a most magnificent (in its simplicity) service. Music was provided by an orchestra of internees who had managed to take their instruments into the camps with them and retain them throughout.

We are getting very busy with Adult Education now. 'Chief' has a class of 18 for maths and 'Guns' (who would by now have a languages degree but for the war) 12 each for English and French and 6 for German. We have also got an Information Room going and are trying to work up some enthusiasm for discussion groups. The first, last evening, was not a success mainly due to Chesney who was leading being so slow 'that he couldn't get out of his own way' as the saying is. However, he volunteered for the job so I must give him a chance....For my part I'm going hard at navigation to get that really consolidated and this evening I've started to build a small wooden office on the bridge for the signalmen to keep all their books and signal files in. We can't get it built officially as its not approved but at Dunstaffnage we wangled the timber and now there is a grand chance to build it and keep idle hands (mine) from mischief. It will be about the size of No. 33's W.C.!! but has of course only a desk in it and a sliding door....

Tomorrow is Tony's birthday. I hope you'll have had a lovely party with Peg [Blanchford's]'s boys [Peter and Nigel] and fine weather in which to enjoy it....When I've finished the office on the bridge I shall probably try and make his wheelbarrow – to use up the fourth wheel of the tricycle which I hope is still at home (the wheel I mean). I have the size of it and will try and make the thing in parts in case I come home by 'transport' and have to cart it across a quarter of the globe (sounds good that!) Have also got to make a stout box for my radio for transport.

October 25th 1945

[initially from Pulo We, off Sumatra, but all posted in the same package so, in effect, a journal covering late October and the start of November]

Well this is a lush tropical island and no mistake. The jungle is dense and profuse and overflowing. Coconut palms, banana plants and all sorts of palms just falling over each other to grow bigger and greener and more lush looking. And some of the beaches are just glorious. Was bathing yesterday afternoon in a cove with pure white coral sand – closed in by massive rocks at each end and the jungle growing right down on the sand fringe. High cliffs were all around with large trees against the skyline and overall bright sunlight and crystal clear sea. Coral of all shapes and sizes and tremendous variety of sea shells of truly lovely colours and no seaweed of any sort anywhere. Such clear clean bathing with a slight surf to give life. Birds of fantastic yellows and reds and immense dragon flies were in and out of the trees and here and there were bright orange red or mauve creeper type flowers. Four of us were driven up there in a Navy car – doing a tour of the island en route. (There is plenty of transport and tons of petrol on the island – left behind by the Japs) It is really a pearl of a place. It is only 35 miles all round the circumference – has 7000 natives and about 120 Europeans (mostly British with a few Dutch – it is a Dutch possession) It has a mountain and a lovely inland lake and lots of inlets and isolated beaches. Money is no use whatever and there is scarcely enough food for the natives so there is nothing else to buy anyway. In fact we as guardship (we are the only Navy ship here) send meat and butter and every other conceivable kind of stores ashore to keep the European element going. Anything from typewriter ribbons to 20 men to clear Jap ammunition dumps. There is no W/T equipment ashore and here again we are the only link they have with the outside world. We lie in the middle of the harbour bay looking as big and efficient as we can and do our best to make life tolerable for the Europeans.

30.10.45

Your letter of October 11th arrived on the 25th – dropped (with some others of course!) by Sunderland flying boat on the Island's airstrip. (Remind me to tell you the story of the Pulo We mail Sunderland) Ships call so infrequently at the Island that all mail is dropped by aircraft. We are now en route Colombo and have all the island's outgoing mail for the past week – as well as a Dutch Army officer, a Naval Doc who will probably come thru to UK with us and three Marines – all as passengers.

We did much good work in the Island I think and also thoroughly enjoyed ourselves. The only British Naval officer there is a grand chap and gave us all the facilities he could and we in turn did our best. Had many lovely trips to the afore-mentioned bathing beach and also sailing (in the whaler) and motor boat trips in the many tree lined coral beached bays near the harbour.

On Sunday three of us were invited to lunch at the Dutch H.Q. on the Island where there are five Dutch officers and the wife and kiddie of the senior one. Most of them were resistance members either in Europe or out here and the wife and kiddie were interned under the Japs for 2 and a half years in Java – the child being 14 days old at the time of internment. The husband had returned to Europe for a time, not knowing where his wife was or even if alive – further they did not hear from each other during the whole separation.

When the Japs started giving in, the husband was sent as senior Dutch officer to Pulo We – still not knowing if his wife was alive, whether he had a son or daughter. Before leaving Columbo he had mentioned to an Air Force (Dutch) friend who was en route to Java that he thought his wife, and he hoped, kiddie were interned there. Should the friend find them – to send them up! And sure enough from the first plane to land on Pulo We airstrip out stepped his 2 and a half year old daughter and his wife. She had had a terrible time and ill treatment and the kiddy was covered in sores – but after nearly a month on Pulo We and the attention of British Navy doctors both are gaining rapidly.

Well we were invited for this RIST TAFEL. To start

with you have several gins and then in comes a plate of split bamboo skewers each with four or five small pieces of pork on it – roasted on the skewers and most luscious. This is eaten by dipping first in a hot (in both senses) sauce and then taking a firm grasp of a piece of pork between the teeth and drawing the skewer out backwards so to speak. Very delicious – and then you sit down to lunch proper which is a large plate of rice and about a dozen fish, egg, meat, root, nut and vegetable dishes to embellish it with. After this came banana fritter and then fruit salad and then coffee with coconut milk. Were we full? The Australian I guess soon went to sleep – we carried on to the beach and in bathing slips only. I went for a long walk along the sands for shells – and after a long interval a bathe!

And now as I said we are en route to Colombo where we are due on the 2nd (when this will be posted) There we shall swop a few bodies no doubt (Cousins is already appointed to another ship out here – he will leave in Ceylon) and after four or five days only, I hope I should be on our way to the U.K.!!! Can you believe it. We are restricted to economical speed these days 10- knots , so we shall be a fair while getting home. If we have no hold-ups we should certainly be in U.K. by Xmas. It would be grand if I could then leave someone else the job of paying off or reducing to Reserve but I guess I shall have to do it....

Glad to read the parcels are beginning to arrive. By this time you should have the shoes and the pyjamas. Do you know if Belhaven got the tea at the same time as yours arrived from Ceylon. Incidentally the two Thermos Flasks and the picnic basket were most useful for the bathing parties at Sabang (Pulo We). I have also a Japanese tea pot – a terrible thing of silver paint and houses and mountains such as grace stalls at Fairs in England – the only trophy I have been able to get hold of. In Pulo We there were dozens of pairs of Japanese binoculars etc. but in spite of the fact that the British were running their town for them, providing the food, medical attention and wireless link with the outside world – the Dutch would not part with a thing. Mean as the devil and most ungracious. Remind me to tell you of them and also the visit of a British officer from the Mainland.

The island of Pulo We is of course just off Sumatra where the Indonesians are so fractious and we were very much 'in the know' of matters political on this Dutch/ Indonesian affair – most interesting.

Tony's wheelbarrow is finished except for painting now. I do hope the wheel is around somewhere at home: if it isn't and you can let me know in time I can make one on board though it won't be so serviceable.

Had a letter from J.W.T.[Jack Thornycroft] thanking me for my 'most informative letter' about their property in Singapore: also went on to ask when I was going to be demobbed 'There will be plenty for you to do when you get back to the firm.'....

31.10.45

Guess I spoke a bit soon about going back very early. Last night we got orders for another (I hope) short job in India but I don't think it will delay us overmuch.

This afternoon is brilliant sunshine and a nice breeze with a kindly sea of glorious blue and we are all on 'A' gun deck either sleeping or writing and it's better than a cruise. I'm feeling fine today again. By the radio you are having foul weather and it must be getting really cold now. Do hope the flat is warm. I think it will be.

The Dutchman is proving most interesting in conversation and looks 100% fitter after only two days at sea. He is getting quite excited at the prospect of having some WRNS and FANY's to talk to in Ceylon as apart from Mrs Harmers there are no white women in Sabang. He is a very pleasant fellow and unlike the rest of them appreciative of what we do for him.

I don't expect to get a lot more mail now as if the programme goes through as planned we shall only be calling at Port Said and Gib and I doubt if mails will catch up with us. So don't be surprised if long intervals occur in my letters from now on.

Have just heard the news of the murder of Brigadier Mallory in Surabaya and the mounting troubles there. Knowing our Dutchman would be interested I told him of it – with a result I shall have to tell you when I get home: just not understandable. I hope you have heard from me sufficiently recently to know I am no longer in that part of the world – nor likely at present to go there unless things get a whole lot worse. I think in fact they will get much better probably – the Indonesians in particular have done themselves untold harm by this outrage. I hope also it will shake public opinion at home that law and order out here is on the wane at present – rather than the reverse.

1.11.45. A few more lines and then will close this to catch the first mail from TRINCOMALEE [Ceylon] where we arrive at dawn tomorrow morning.

The Dutchman is sitting in my cabin at present having come up to listen to the news – and have a nightcap too. He is really quite appreciative of our hospitality on his trip over and has just given us his address in Amsterdam so that if I am ever in Holland after the war 'he can return the very nice hospitality he has received on board.'

Shall be at TRINCO for a few days and am taking the opportunity to get the ship ready (boiler clean etc) for the run home (I hope). Surprising with what a will the E.R. staff turn to now on a job which in normal times they would be aghast to have to do; boiler cleans are usually (in war) done by shore based people of course. Now the ship's staff are only too keen to ensure a quick run home without mechanical hitch!...

The Home Front 1942–1946

In general, apart from Virginia who moved around Britain with the WAAF, the women stayed at home, much of the time not knowing where their menfolk were. Nevertheless it is surprising how frequent the letters were, and how efficient the postal service, whether from ships at sea, shore bases, or home. The censors, too, must have done their best to maintain a fast throughput. Only in the tense days leading up to the invasion (D-Day) were there serious restrictions on travel and communication: for a few months, all travel to coastal towns was banned and there were no trunk calls allowed between mainland Britain and the whole of Ireland (these were in any case restricted to six minutes). On 23 March 1944 Maureen writes to Grace, 'It seems to me from now on you are going to be the lucky one when this ban comes into force. It is going to be awful if Bill is based somewhere in England or Scotland & to know we cannot see each other maybe for the duration. Virginia and Desmond will not be allowed over either. This is how poor "loyal Ulster" must suffer for other people's sins!'

As it turned out, her worst fears were not realised. They were in touch until a few days before D-Day, and he was on leave in

Belfast shortly after, as we have seen. Apart from the usual dangers attendant on active service there were no serious worries about being parted for a lengthy period until 3 August 1944, when Maureen is optimistic that the war cannot last much longer, 'but how I pray that Bill won't be sent off to fight the Japs.' This time she was not so lucky, as that is exactly what happened: though the fighting was over by the time his ship reached the Far East, he was away from July 1945 until January 1946.

Much of the correspondence concerns accommodation, holidays and travel. Bill and Maureen's first home together, the flat in Edinburgh, was spacious and comfortable, though relations with the landlady had their ups and downs: one night Maureen got into terrible hot water for burning three lights instead of one, regarded by Mrs Harley as unpardonably extravagant when everyone was supposed to be saving fuel. During this time she worked at packing parcels for the Red Cross, presumably to earn some money to defray the rent. Grace managed to visit her there in September 1942, quite an expedition from Surrey. Later on, when she became pregnant, Maureen moved back home, after an extended stay through April and May at 'The Lupins' hotel in Weymouth, Bill being by then stationed at nearby Portland.

On one occasion, she stood at a prearranged spot on the shore while he sailed by, Morse code flashing from the bridge – but of course she could not understand the message he was attempting to convey!

Through the invasion period she was in comparative safety in Belfast, preparing for Tony's birth, and afterwards there was

Wartime picnic

a nurse as well as help from Harriet, the maid, by now an indispensable member of the household. June 1944 saw her on holiday in Bundoran, Co. Donegal with her father. They were able to relax, fishing, walking and going on long cycle rides together, while the baby was being looked after at 'Belhaven' by her mother and Harriet. In August, Grace was expected to join her and Bill on another holiday at a house they had taken in Ballycastle, Co. Antrim, when she would see Tony for the first time. Fortunately, 'Harriet's home is at Ballycastle, & as she is going up for the weekend, we will travel together & she will be a great help. A bicycle, pram, cot, playpen, wireless, luggage & Tony would be a bit of a job on my own.'

Everything was of course harder to come by than before the war, and there is much exchanging of clothing coupons, hunting for wool, and generally becoming used to the necessity to 'make do and mend'. For Christmas 1944 Maureen 'made some utility almond paste, and it was quite a success!' Eggs were so scarce that it was seen as worth the risk of sending them through the post, even though one such attempt resulted in five out of the dozen arriving broken. Dressmaking expertise was at a premium, especially with a young child: as he grew, his clothes had to be adapted or made up from something else. The gift from Grace of a subscription to *Housewife* magazine was much appreciated by the young bride. Although they 'had fun cooking and lighting fires' when Harriet was off, Maureen was probably conscious of the need to hone her domestic skills, in preparation for a future life in England without domestic help.

Meanwhile, in Kingston and around London, Grace and Dorothy were enduring the air raids and their consequences. Letters from them describe their own experience of the Blitz in September and October 1940. Dorothy was surprised at how little damage was apparent in the main streets of the West End, but of course things were very different in East London. The area around Grace's block of flats on Kingston Hill was regularly hit, with ruptured gas and water mains, windows blown in, and fires started by incendiary bombs. She took her share of duty as an ARP warden, as well as holding down a demanding job involving the distribution of clothing and other supplies to, it appears, soldiers and refugees. Her flat being at the top of the building,

> I go down every night and sleep in Mrs Holman's [ground floor] flat, coming up for the 'All Clear' & as the 'Gerries' work almost like clockwork I can normally reckon on being in my own bed by 6 o'c. Usually we start getting

> noisy about 20.02 or 20.32 & he goes steadily on till 05.30 to 06.30, not bad going on his part, but surprisingly little damage...Vivien [Maughling] seems to be having the time of her life putting out incendiary bombs. She put out about 14 the other night. Also the old man was darting in and out of a house next door which was on fire . They are all behaving extremely well...'Clara' is just sounding (Don't you think 'Mona' for the alert and 'Clara' for the 'All Clear' rather good.)

Long after the air raid threat appeared to have receded, and when the war seemed to be drawing to a close, the civilian population received a nasty shock in the form of flying bombs (V-1s or 'doodle bugs'). Raids using this new weapon began in June 1944, in direct retaliation for the D-Day invasion. It was the last throw of 'that archfiend', as Lottie called Hitler in one of her letters. 'It is a terrible strain for you all, & that diving under the table all the time must be the very divel on stockings and clothes, as well as being most uncomfortable', wrote Maureen, as so often feeling bad about living an almost normal life in Northern Ireland while they were still suffering in England. She also refers to the danger of infections, including TB, spreading amongst children in the shelters.

In November 1944 she hopes 'that as soon as the V2s stop, Tony and I will be moving over, tho' of course it will be very sad leaving home, but more & more I find I want a place of our own, and of course Bill is just aching for it. To-night I heard on the wireless that there are over a million young couples who will soon be needing homes, & there is nothing to meet the demand, so feel we must not be amongst the million!' By this time, plans for moving into a flat in Cromwell Court were well advanced. Initially, they were to share Grace's flat, before transferring to their own on the ground floor. At the end of the year Maureen was worried about bringing Tony into unnecessary danger while the flying bombs were still falling, but Allied forces had overrun the last V-1 launching sites within range of England by the end of October so there was nothing to fear from them. A few of the advanced rocket-driven V-2s fell after that, but caused very few casualties. Owing to security restrictions, there was often a time-lag between developments, both good and bad, occurring and news of them reaching the general public.

Finally, on 24 April 1945, Maureen writes in detail about arrangements for transferring herself, Tony, and various goods and chattels from Belfast to Kingston. She is relieved that Grace

Cromwell Court, 1948. Waiting for King George VI and Queen Elizabeth to pass on their way to open the new power station at Kingston. Seward flats on ground and second floors in the corner behind the little boy with the cap (Tony?).

has opted for 'the larger flat' (Number 33 Cromwell Court) for them to share, and that her mother will be coming with her to help with the move. We can assume that they were living in the flat by early in May.

In July 1946 Maureen, Bill and Tony were on a fortnight's holiday at Weymouth, once again staying at 'The Lupins'. My very first memory is of splashing in the sea there and being paddled by Bill on a hired 'fun-float', two wooden floats joined together by thin planks which served as seats (some years later he and I constructed one of our own in the garage of our house at Epsom). Maureen's letter to her mother of 15 July confirms that the weather was as perfect as I remember it to have been. In the same letter she gives the long-awaited news that they should be moving into the ground-floor flat the following week. So, by the end of July 1946, we were firmly ensconced in our own home at last – 18 Cromwell Court, Kingston Hill.

Tony 'driving' a steamroller, 1948. It was laying new tarmac at Cromwell Court.

6 Recovering Past Time: A Visit to 'Belhaven'

One day, on a visit to Belfast in 2005, I returned to the site of 1, Deramore Park South. Nothing remained. The old house had been torn down and replaced by a small block of flats, so there was nothing to show to my daughters and nephews who were with me. It seemed to have been unfairly singled out for oblivion since, as far as I could tell, all the other large houses in the road, with their extensive gardens, remained. So 'Belhaven' exists now only in the memories of the few of us remaining, who shared its life with those who are long departed. And yet, perhaps, this fate is preferable to its lingering on, subject to more mundane uses (it was for a while a dentist's surgery), or the indignity of being split up into apartments. The way of life it embodied faded away rapidly with the demise of the textile industry which had sustained it. By the 1960s my generation of Belfast cousins had already started moving away from troubled Ulster to the mainland, and Ewart's had ceased to be a manufacturing entity by the end of that decade. The memories evoked in this chapter relate mainly to the early 1950s, when I was aged between 7 and 12.

Following the deaths of Nina in 1968, and Victor in 1972, the house was put up for sale. It must have survived as a private residence at least until 1978, when an advertisement described it as a 'Delightful gentleman's residence set in gardens extending to some one acre'. Allowing for estate agent hyperbole, this was no more than the truth. As far back as 1863, the corporation minutes had noted that the Malone area to the south of the city had become a preferred location for the wealthy and influential. Besides the status conferred by its proximity to Queen's College and the Botanic Gardens, it had practical advantages: the area is on a gravel ridge which helped to keep it free from flooding.[35] It was not entirely free from problems of subsidence, however, as every Spring Victor was to be seen up a ladder, carefully monitoring the progress of a crack which had appeared in one of the walls.

The house was built between 1890 and 1914, when this area of substantial suburban villas was developed on farmland bordering the east side of the Malone Road. It belongs to the latter part of the period, when fashions began to change from High

Top: 'Belhaven' north front; below, 'Belhaven' from the south

Victorian formality towards designs influenced by Edwardian Arts and Crafts.[36] 'Belhaven' was constructed of dark red brick, with Arts and Crafts touches including half-timbering, several gables, and an asymmetrical layout. The impressive if antediluvian fittings in the bathroom adjoining Nina's bedroom – including a shower with multiple jets coming at the user from both sides as well as above – suggested late Victorian or Edwardian luxury. After living in at least two rented properties for a while after their return from the US, Victor and Nina and their children probably took possession of 'Belhaven' in the late 1920s.

Aspect

The house was built on a north-facing rise, with front steps leading up to a large sunny porch; the dining room is to its left

Maureen, Victor and Nina, 28 May 1940

in the top photograph opposite. The bow window at far left belonged to the formal drawing room. To the right of the porch was the kitchen and 'offices'. On the upper floors there were nine bedrooms, three bathrooms, a play room and a box room, with extensive attics on the top floor.

To the rear, there was a fine conservatory, initially, as shown opposite, separate from the house but later linked by a small sun room. The bow window to the left belonged to the morning room, which looked out on a rockery. Family photographs tended to be taken here as it was the sunniest and most sheltered spot.

Behind the rockery was a tennis court laid out on a terrace; overhung by the neighbours' trees, it was rather damp and shady. Further to the east on a steep slope was the vegetable garden, notable for its delicious broad beans and abundance of sweet peas, pumping out their heady scent. At the foot of this slope was the '3-car' garage and oil-fired heating plant.

The 'Station Wagon', Maureen and Virginia aboard.

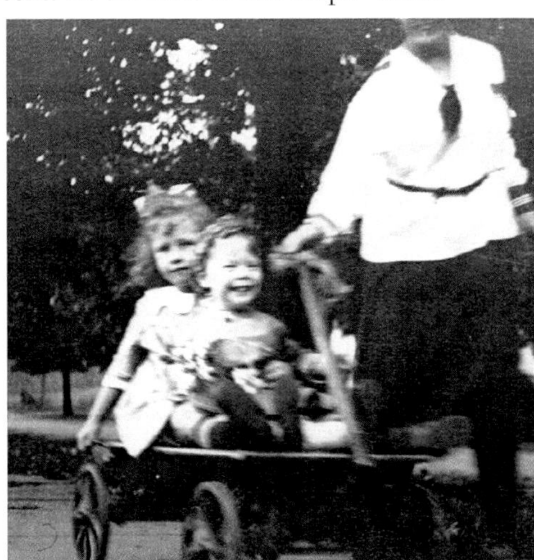

A challenge I set myself was to ride the old 'Station Wagon' from the top of the slope, down the path by the compost heap, along the side of the garage and to the drive beyond, if possible building enough momentum to take me out as far as the road. There were many obstacles on the way and 95 per cent of the time I hit one and fell off, but the occasional 'clear run' was a cause for celebration. This

A later view of the front and east, showing (left) the sun room linking the house to the conservatory
Below: Sweep and front gate, c.1930

vehicle originated in America and was a thing of beauty. It was, I suppose, a luxury version of the soapbox carts that less privileged children used to construct from a wooden crate and old pram wheels. Painted red and black, sturdily built, with front wheels on a swivel connected to the steering stick, and a somewhat ineffectual brake on one back wheel operated with the left hand, it could reach a dizzying speed. The wheels were metal-rimmed, and rumbled along on the asphalt paths. Like Citizen Kane's sledge 'Rosebud', it was probably my first love.

A tunnel of roses, trained over an iron framework, led from the garage to the house. This picture was taken in winter so there are none in flower, but their absence enables one to see the windows of the sun room to the left.

To complete this survey, the view below is from the front towards the sweep and the gate out into the road. To the right was a large lawn and herbaceous border, taking up the space between here and the drive into the garage . Nina has written on the back, 'Our fleet of cars. Desmond is able to drive now but only on very rare occasions with Vic or myself beside him. Note

the big "carry-all" on the back of the big car that contains 2 big suitcases.' All these early photographs would have been sent to her mother in America to give her an idea of the new house.

Many rooms

Internally, the house was spacious, comfortable and welcoming, with a multitude of fascinating nooks and crannies (I still dream occasionally of finding rooms tucked away that I hadn't known were there). This impression was reinforced by the slightly eccentric layout: while there were ostensibly only two main floors, it seemed as if there were several more, as a number of rooms were built at mezzanine levels between floors, leading off the main staircase. It may be that these rooms, located as they all were above the kitchen area, were not part of the original house but added later; one of them was Harriet's bedroom and another a spare bedroom reserved for the use of additional temporary staff or helpers who were drafted in from time to time. At the highest level were the mysterious attics, one used as a store room (kept firmly under lock and key), one a lumber room, and a third a billiard room (later demoted to another lumber room full of unexpected treasures: my favourite was the old musical box from Maralin Rectory, eventually passed to me and now fully refurbished and in good working order).

The entrance hall was dominated by a large and resonant gong, which Harriet used to summon us to meals. In the dining room to the left was a large bow window, with aspidistra, where Nicky, the Cairn terrier, used to sit in wait for visitors to the front door, barking himself hoarse every time one appeared. On cold days the gas fire sighed gently, its fake coals enhanced by (highly dangerous) flakes of asbestos, which glowed satisfyingly. Above the fireplace was a watercolour of Victor's yacht in full sail. The next doorway led into the drawing room, furnished for show rather than use, with polished parquet floor and touches of gilt and ormolu. This had become little more than a passageway to the cosy little sunroom and the conservatory beyond – but it did house a baby grand piano, so occasionally functioned as a music room, mainly when Desmond dropped in and played a piece or two.

Near the foot of the staircase (down whose banisters one could slide from the top of the house to the bottom) was the doorway into the morning room. This was very snug, with well-worn old furniture, a small library, and a print of 'When did you last see your father?' on the wall by the fireplace. (How affecting, and popular, was this scene of pretty Cavalier children being interrogated by a stern Roundhead). It was Nina's space, where she spent most time after she became invalided with osteo-arthritis (although she would usually move to the sunroom later on fine days). For us and our parents, she was 'Momma', and Victor 'Poppa', so I shall henceforth refer to them thus, now that these reminiscences have reached my own lifetime. Momma (like Virginia) was a heavy smoker, and one of my tasks was to pop down to the shops on Maureen's old bicycle to replenish her supply of Gallahers cigarettes. These came in two strengths: the milder variety in green packets, the extra strength in dark blue, and I would be instructed to buy some combination of the two. At the same time Harriet would usually ask me to pick up some groceries (on account, of course) from Mr Rainey's shop on the Lisburn Road.

If Harriet or I wished to go into town, either singly or together, we would take one of the trams which plied along the centre of the Malone Road, conveniently stopping opposite the turning to Deramore Park South. Ah! those trams, with their shining wood- and brass-work, smooth ride and sheer convenience. Bells ringing, they would convey you in style to the city centre, past the Botanic Gardens and the leafy avenues – one named 'Sans Souci Park' – where resided the prosperous Belfast bourgeoisie. To a child it did indeed seem a world 'without care'.

Household management

At the end of the passage beyond the morning room was the swing door leading to Harriet's domain. Here she presided over a scullery, a pantry, a washroom and a walled and tiled yard, open to the sky, where laundry hung out to dry. But the focal point of this complex was the large, light kitchen, always warm, for here was the boiler and range. It was a different world from that on the other side of the swing door. The radio was always on, tuned to the Light Programme; 'wee Peter', Harriet's budgie (who would daintily take morsels from her mouth) flitted about; tradesmen gossiped through the window; and no-one had to be on their best behaviour. Often Harriet's brother Paddy – large, kind and slow – and her big sister Annie – always ready with a vigorous hug – were visiting. Paddy loved to share his cigarettes, and Annie liked to tease, in a joshing kind of way. Both often helped out with tasks in the house and garden. Harriet's large

Catholic family was based in Ballycastle, Co. Antrim – 'good, country people' as she always said – where her sister May ran their farm after her husband was killed in an accident. In the aftermath of this tragedy Harriet wrote (January 1957),

> ...and indeed my thoughts were with poor May & the children at home the first Christmas without their daddy. however she wasn't forgotten as Bobs cousin in Armoy 6 miles from Ballycastle. they have a big grocer shop & butcher shop. they sent her a big Christmas hamper.a big roast of meat cake Biscuits tea. fruit and chocolates for the children. and on Christmas night didn't 2 mother pigs have Babies which kept them very busy in all the snow. one pig had 11. the other 8. and May and Annie had to sit with the mother pigs from 6 o'clock in the evening until 9.30. and bring the wee pigs into the warm kitchen for the night to keep them warm. so that kept her from thinking.

Harriet Barton was originally engaged as a young housemaid when there were several servants, but by the time we knew her she was housemaid, cook, nurse and essentially manager of the household, under Momma's supervision. There was a gardener, and when there were visiting children she might have some additional temporary help, but no other staff. All through our childhood she was a constant loving presence, and when Momma and Poppa became old and frail, she looked after them to the end. Her cooking was of a piece with herself, full of care and thought. One of her signature touches was to separate the cream from gold-top milk and present it in a little jug for each of us to add to our porridge; and she excelled in producing tempting delicacies for anyone who was ill. Her Irish soda bread, done on the griddle, was a particular treat.

Harriet and Nicky

To the children she wrote letters, sent presents, flattered us, and boosted our self-confidence. She wrote exactly as she spoke, with much amusing gossip as well as concern for our welfare. Here is one cameo, in a letter to Maureen ('the Commander' is Brian Magee, Virginia's husband):

> ...Belinda. she is a sweet wee girl. and loves Nicky. I would just love to have her all the time...the Commander is a great

> healp about the house. he does all the washing up. and would set the table if I was busy. and very good at making his Breakfast on Sunday mornings while I was at Mass. and doing beds. I would hurry up to give him a hand. I have them done Harriet. Yes says Mrs Magee. he thinks so. but when I get into [?] at bed time I don't know what the right end of the clothes is: anyway I told Mrs Magee how much I would miss him. well you can't have him as I would miss him too. it was good having them over the Holidays. if it was just for the Mistress alone. it cheers her up. as the day is so long sitting by the fire when you can't get out.

And this to Momma, convalescing in hospital:

> A Happy Easter to you this morning Madam dear. thank God you are much better than at this time last year...get the Master to tell you I sent Dr. Arnold flowers he dosn't tell you half the news I tell him to tell you...I wish you were here and the birds are nesting. the Robin is working on his above the kitchen window. Peter is in good form and loves to empty his seed lid over the side of the tray where he sits. walks along with it in his mouth untill he gets to the edge and loves to let it go. and as much as anything loves to hear me give out to him. Oh Peter what did you do oh. your a bad wee boy.

And finally, a flash of wit at the height of the Troubles, in October 1971:

> I would have loved to have a night out on the slates but just not at the moment as I would have been taken as a sniper.

(It was not always so: before the sectarian tensions erupted in 1968, she used to take me down to the Lisburn Road on the 'Glorious Twelfth' of July to watch the Orange bands in procession: to many Catholics like her at the time this was merely an innocent spectacle, without sinister political overtones. Poppa would joke about the 'very loyal people around here', as we drove past the crowds around the bonfires on Sandy Row the night before, burning 'ould red socks' (the Pope) in effigy.)

She was assiduous in attending Mass, but her greatest pleasure was to go dancing on her days off. We nearly lost her when a man she had met asked her to marry him. It must have been an agonising decision, but in the end she could not quite bring herself to go through with it. She adored Momma – 'What a woman!'– and genuinely could not bear to leave the family. Poppa made provision for her to have a house and pension in her old age, but initially, after first Momma and then he had died, she spent a number of years looking after other old people, living with them as companion and nurse.

Journey and arrival

Our annual excursions to Belfast began with the long drive from Surrey to Birkenhead, where we left the car with a Thornycroft contact of Bill's, a Mr Gilmour, who would then drive us through the Mersey tunnel (all that water above us – how exciting!) to the Liverpool docks. There we would embark, always in the evening, on one of the Belfast Steamship Company's ferries.

Up the gangplank we went into a strange other world, of passages, cabins and stairways, with a special, indefinable smell, of which the main components seemed to be freshly laundered linen, polish, and a faint hint of engine oil. There we were greeted by smartly uniformed staff and directed down to our cabins. The picture overleaf suggests more luxurious berths than I remember, but they were comfortable enough, and we usually managed to secure one with a porthole. Once safely stowed, there was time to explore the ship, and watch the preparations for casting off. I was usually in bed by the time the ship got under way, but remember how it seemed to take hours to go through various locks, down the Mersey and out into the open sea. With all the excitement, sleep was limited, and it was important to be up in time to see the Isle of Man dropping astern, the Irish coast looming up before us, then the stately progress up Belfast Lough, with

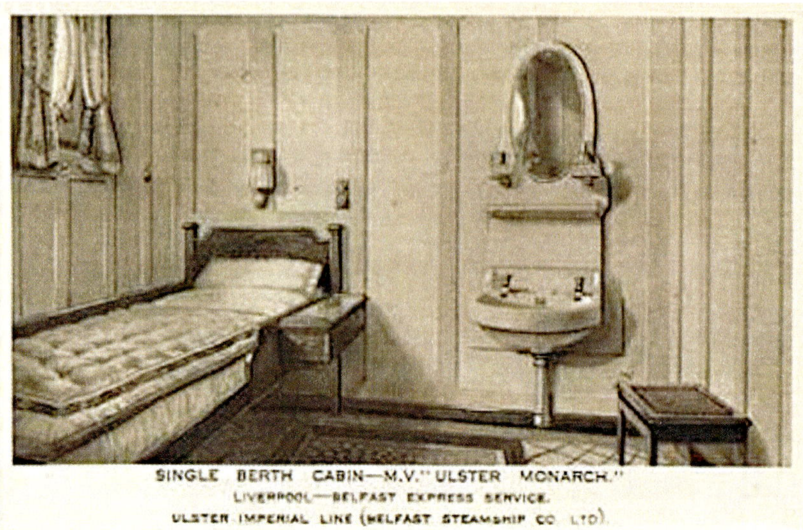

the green hills and little towns and villages on either side. This was followed by the drama of arrival, great ropes and cables being flung from ship to shore, and the shouts of the dock workers in their unfamiliar Ulster dialect.

Once off the ship, we were met by a Ewart's car and driver, who would whisk us up to 'Belhaven', where an enormous Union Jack was run out on a flagpole above the entrance to welcome us. Hugs and kisses all round, followed by Harriet's splendid breakfast and the warmth of the dining room fire. We had arrived! 'Belhaven' would be our base for two or three happy weeks of catching up with the relations, visits to the country and the seaside, walks along the Lagan a few fields away, and, in later years, longer excursions of several days to Virginia and Brian's house in beautiful Donegal.

7 Epilogue

It seems appropriate to bring this account to a close with the advent of a new generation during and after the war. If the First World War created 'a crack across the table of history', in Ford Madox Ford's phrase, the Second equally ushered in a new world. For Britain, the supreme achievement of the Attlee government in creating the welfare state was balanced by a rapid decline in the nation's power and influence in the world. With the sudden cancellation of Lend-Lease by our American allies, the country became virtually bankrupt overnight, and was reliant on a massive loan from the US to survive. Never again would we have the global reach which enabled us to fight across so many theatres of war.

In trade, we could no longer rely on easy access to the markets of the Empire. Fierce competition arose from newly energised countries, often the supposed 'losers' in the conflict, who were able to rebuild from scratch with massive investments from the victors, the most notable being the Marshall Plan. It is a familiar story which does not need to be rehearsed here, and it will be no surprise that the two venerable firms, with whose fates those of the family had been so closely linked for generations, partook in the general decline.

Ewart's had been losing market for decades, as damask became less fashionable for table settings, and easy-care fabrics were developed for clothing. There had also been persistent criticism that the designs used on Irish linen were old-fashioned and unattractive. Although Ewart's had developed capacity in man-made fibres, it was no match for the cheaper product being manufactured in Asia and other developing regions. Exacerbating all these problems, from 1968 Northern Ireland was plunged into the 'Troubles', making business activity of all kinds difficult, and new investment increasingly hard to come by. Plants closed and thousands of workers were laid off. In 1973, Ewart's manufacturing interests were merged with those of another leading Belfast linen manufacturer, William Liddell, to create Ewart Liddell Holdings Ltd, in which the large English textile group Vantona held a majority share. It was promised at the time that the Glenbank Bleaching Works would be reopened and up to 1,000 jobs saved across the combined company, but little came of this. Ewart's as an independent entity was reduced to a property company, Ewart New Northern Ltd, administering the firm's portfolio of offices and factories. This too virtually disappeared over the next few years, through a further process of merger and acquisition. Mercifully, Victor did not survive to see the final humiliation, dying in 1972. Nevertheless, after such a rich and fulfilling life as one of the leading citizens of Belfast, culminating in the award of the CBE in 1954 for his services to the linen industry, his last years must have been deeply saddened by the decline of the company to which he had devoted his career.

Thornycroft's last years followed a similar pattern of postwar depression, followed by a merger with its main rival, Vosper. Bill did not live to see this development, which took place a few months after his death in 1966, although he must have known it was coming. In fact, he might well have welcomed it, as he often commented to me how crazy it was that the two companies were so often bidding against each other for key foreign contracts. The outcome here was more positive than in the case of Ewart's, the new merged company of Vosper Thornycroft successfully combining the resources of two companies, each with over 100 years' experience of ship and boatbuilding, for both military and private customers. Further mergers in turn absorbed the new company over the years, but the core business remains, with many of the original yards still working.

What did these changes mean for our generation? Ewart's and Thornycroft's had provided a good living for our parents and a reasonably prosperous middle-class lifestyle, with private education taken for granted as the norm. Thus equipped, we were able to make our way in the new world of the 1960s and beyond. The major difference was that there was no longer the option of continuing in the tradition of following parents and grandparents into a long-established family firm. As for so many British families, a career in manufacturing industry became a rarity rather than a first choice, and nearly all of us found ourselves working in services, commerce or the professions: teaching, nursing, social work, hospitality, publishing, accountancy.

As always, change has brought both gains and losses for family life. The old, close-knit relationships across many branches of a large family no longer obtain, so it is a colder, more individualistic world. For all the incredible developments in communication it could be said that contact across generations and different branches is less than it was. On the other hand, we are more free to lead our own lives without constant reference to what our relatives may think of our choices. But this too marks loss as much as gain, since, while we interfere less in each other's lives, perhaps we care less, not being so involved.

'*Si je les perd je suis perdu*' – 'If I lose them, I am lost'. In attempting to set down the story of my family over several generations I have been guided by the belief that it matters, and that our forebears deserve to be remembered and honoured. No-one writes letters nowadays, so we may be the last generation able to draw on an archive of written texts in hard copy, to help us in recreating the very different worlds of our ancestors. The human desire to be remembered is unlikely to disappear, and our children will no doubt find other ways of leaving their mark, possibly by preserving some kind of 'digital legacy' to pass on to their children. Let us hope so.

Appendix 1

The Seward Family

William Seward, d.1815
master mariner
m.1790 Sarah Rendell, 1765-1843

William John, 1791-1858
Master of the Emigrants Depot, Plymouth
m. 4 times:(1) and (2) unknown
(3) Ann Rendell, d. 1830
(4) Mary Pike, d.1861

William Rendell, 1816-1884
station master
m. 1838 Charlotte Poe Renell, 1811-1897

Hadassah, 1822-?
m. William R. WEBBER, 1806-1888,
carver and gilder, later worked at Emigrants Depot, Plymouth

William John Seward Webber
1842-c.1919 *sculptor*

Samuel Henry Rendell
carpenter, emigrated to Australia 1859
m. 1841 Elizabeth Letitia Lishman, who d.1904

Elizabeth milliner
m. ? LISLE, 1846

Susan, d.1846

Elizabeth Renell (Rennie), 1843-?
m. William Richard LISLE,
goldsmith and clockmaker

William Renell, 1845-188?
railway engineer
m. Sarah ('Etta') Elliott, 1852-1938

Hadassah Julia ('**Dass**'),
1850-?

Ann Rendell (Nance), 1856-?

Charlotte Cecilia Hadassah (Lottie),
1876-1963 m. Hubert BLANCHFORD,
1874-1960, *stained glass artist*

William Thomas Renell, 1880-1928
engineer m. 1906
Grace Florence Edwards, 1886-1978

Ralph Renell, 1883-1970
engineer
m. Wyn Cannon

Compiled by Tony Seward, December 2018

- **Hubert Noel**, 1907-1993 *banker*
  m. Evelyn McNeill, 1908-1985
  - **Penelope**, 1942 -
    m. Douglas ALDRICH-BLAKE
  - **Gillian**, 1944-
    m. Donald HIND
  - **Robert**, 1957-
- **Brian Seward**, 1909-1993
  Captain RN m. Peggy Taylor,
  1908-1997
  - **Peter**, 1942- 2010, OBE,
    Commander RN
    m. Erica Johnston, 1941-2008
  - **Nigel**, 1944-
    m. Lynette Lanchbery
- **Bridget Mary**, 1916-
  schoolteacher
  m. John HARVEY WEBB
  - **James**, 1942-
  - **Noel Seward**, 1942-
  - **Elizabeth Renell**, 1944-
    m. Martin WIGGINS, d.

- **Dorothy Grace**, 1909-1958 *journalist*
  m. 1939 Thomas Robertson (Bob) KIDD,
  businessman, d.1983
  - **John William**, 1947-
- **William Renell**, 1912-1966 *engineer*
  m. 1942 Maureen Cecil Clarendon,
  1915-2000
  - **Anthony William Renell**, 1943-
    m.1968 Angela Gail Wilmot, 1947-
    - **Miranda Caroline**, 1973-
      m. 2002 Glenn HAYWARD, 1973-
      - **Oliver Andrew**, 2006-
      - **Toby James**, 2009-
    - **Katherine Elizabeth**, 1977-
      m. 2003 James McLEISH, 1974-
      - **Emily Alice**, 2007-
  - **Jennifer**, b. and d. 1947
  - **Timothy Clarendon**, 1949-2001
    m. 1983 Elizabeth Anne Debnam,1952-
    - **William Debnam**, 1983-
    - **Ralph James**, 1988-
  - **Jeremy Philip**, 1953-1973

- **Howard**, m. Maria Rittinger.
- **James**, m. Susan Tyte.

Appendix 2

The British naval blockade and convoy system during the Napoleonic Wars

The main incentive for merchantmen like the *Jubilee* to join convoys was a reduction of 30% in insurance premiums for convoyed ships. As late as 1814 there was still a danger of being attacked by French or American 'commerce raiders', as the following account makes clear.

The British blockade of Brest had resumed in 1805, immediately after the breakdown of the Peace of Amiens, and continued until 1815, effectively keeping the French Channel fleet out of the war. Its consequent failure to link up with the French and Spanish Mediterranean fleets under Admiral Villeneuve was a major contributing factor to Nelson's victory at Trafalgar on 21 October 1805. However, the blockade meant that the British Western fleet had to maintain station in the Bay of Biscay (a notoriously stormy stretch of water) on a lee shore during westerly gales. When these blew the British fleet had to take shelter in the nearest sheltered anchorage – Torbay. This allowed some French ships to break the blockade as the gale died down and before the British could return.

The main French fleet could not avail itself of such opportunities as the capital ships were in a very run-down condition and their crews, if they had any, lacked the sea-time experience to be able to handle and fight their ships. However, frigates and other smaller craft could and did escape the blockade, and once out their main task was commerce raiding. Hence the need for British merchantmen to be convoyed. In addition to the relatively few frigates and other French naval ships, French privateers were also active. These operated from many French ports, the main one in France being Dunkirk, and in the Caribbean Guadeloupe. Thus there were threats from both sides of the Atlantic. An added danger was hostility from the Americans, who were at war with Britain from 1812 onwards.

Nigel Blanchford
Editor, *Topmasts. The Newsletter of the Society for Nautical Research*

Appendix 3

VFC – the public man

Victor Frederick Clarendon became chairman of the board of Ewart's in 1950. He retired in 1967 after 60 years with the company, to be succeeded by Sir Ivan Ewart (with eye patch, below).

On 8 August 1961, Ewart's head office and warehouse in Bedford Street were honoured by a visit from the Queen and the Duke of Edinburgh, who had arrived in Belfast that morning on the Royal Yacht *Britannia*. They were greeted at the entrance by VFC and the Directors, and taken on a tour of the premises. Ewart's was the only commercial enterprise thus singled out on this visit. Overleaf is a selection of photographs recording the event, clearly enjoyed by all concerned, not least the loyal and enthusiastic members of staff!

As well as being associated for many years with a number of bodies connected with the linen industry, VFC devoted a large part of his life to public service in Belfast. He was honorary

Moments from the Queen and the Duke of Edinburgh's visit to Ewart's.

Opposite: Victor, Tony and Maureen in London for VFC's investiture.

treasurer of the Royal Victoria Hospital for 21 years, and a member of the Senate of Queen's University. He became chairman of the RVH management committee until it merged with the Belfast Hospital Management Committee in 1947. He also served as chairman of the Belfast Chamber of Commerce, chairman of the Linen Trade Advisory Committee, and Deputy Lieutenant (DL) for the County Borough of Belfast.

His obituaries in *The Belfast Newsletter* and *The Belfast Telegraph* (following his death on 28 October 1972) stated that it was mainly for his services to the hospital and university that he was awarded the CBE (Commander of the Order of the British Empire) in the 1954 New Year Honours List. The investiture, by Queen Elizabeth the Queen Mother at Buckingham Palace, took place on 23 February 1954. Maureen and I (aged 10) were present on this memorable occasion.

His outside interests included shooting and fishing, sailing, golf and gardening. Beautiful words and music would move him to tears: like the passage from the King James Bible where Ruth refuses to be parted from her widowed mother-in-law Naomi:

> … whither thou goest, I will go; and where thou lodgest, I will lodge: thy people shall be my people, and thy God my God. Where thou diest, will I die; and there I will be buried: the Lord do so to me, and more also, if aught but death part thee and me.

As a grandfather, he was affectionate, funny and encouraging ('Well done, sporty boy!'), with an occasional touch of irascibility to season his usual bonhomie. In his later years, we are told, he sought to bring 'help and comfort to the elderly and infirm, whom he visited personally in their homes, throughout the community'.

References

1 'Grace's Guide. British Industrial History', www.gracesguide.co.uk/William_Ewart_and_Son, accessed 03/01/2018, to which I owe much of the information concerning the early history of the company.

2 'Irish Linen. An account of its processes of manufacture, incorporating the history of William Ewart and Son Limited Belfast', 1950, revised and updated 1964 to mark the 150th anniversary of the company's foundation.

3 Richard Froggatt, *Dictionary of Ulster Biography*, www.newulsterbiography.co.uk, accessed 03/01/2018.

4 Quoted in S.J.Connolly (ed.) *Belfast 400. People Place and History*, Liverpool University Press, 2012, p.207. Connolly, *passim*, is the main source for this brief summary of the history of the Belfast linen industry.

5 William Topping, quoted in Connolly, p.211.

6 From Seamus Heaney, *Death of a Naturalist*, Faber, 1966.

7 Froggatt, *op.cit.*

8 C.S.Lewis, *Surprised by Joy. The Shape of My Early Life*, Geoffrey Bles, 1955; Fontana paperback edition 1959, pp. 41-3.

9 *ibid.* p.64.

10 *Directory of Irish Architects, 1720-1940*, www.dia.ie/architects/view/1035/CLARENDON-FREDERICKVILLIERS, accessed 10/01/2018.

11 *Like an Evening Gone. Written to mark the Centenary of the Church of the Holy and Undivided Trinity, Magheralin, 1891-1991.* Compiled by Mrs Eileen Cousins, BA, 1991. Printed by Banbridge Chronicle Press Ltd. Or see website: laeg.tripod.com/html/5.htm.

12 *ibid.* Or see website: laeg.tripod.com/html/3.htm.

13 *ibid.*

14 Letter of 27/01/1966.

15 *Proceedings and Transactions of the Kilkenny and South-East of Ireland Archaeological Society*, Vol III, 1854-5, Dublin, 1856, fn 1, pp.273-4.

16 Alice Mauger, 'Confinement of the Higher Orders': The Social Role of Private Lunatic Asylums in Ireland, c.1820–60', *Journal of the History of Medicine and Allied Sciences*, Vol. 67, No. 2, April 2012, pp. 281-317, Oxford Academic.

17 http://strangeco.blogspot.co.uk/2013/10/the-witch-of-staten-island.html, posted 7/10/2013, accessed 17/1/2018.

18 Marguerite M. Rivas, email and attachments addressed to Victor R. Clarendon, 06/01/2003.

19 Lewis, *op.cit.* pp.45-9.

20 'Genealogical Table of the Ewarts of Northern Ireland'. Compiled by Wiclif McCready, BA, FRCSI, 20 College Gardens, Belfast, September, 1929. Copies are held by several members of the family.

21 From https://www.historyextra.com/period/georgian/the-real-history-behind-poldark-series-three-episode-five/

22 Transcripts emailed to me by Peter Blanchford on 23 February 2000.

23 Information about the Emigrant Depots in the following paragraphs is taken from two websites:
http://www.historic-shipping.co.uk/Emigration/theemigrationdepot.html
<u>and</u> https://www.britishempire.co.uk/article/plymouth/emigrationdepot.htm

24 For full details of W.J.S.Webber's life and works, see: https://sculpture.gla.ac.uk/view/person.php?id=msib4_1256301512. There are two copies of this bust, one currently with my sister-in-law Elizabeth Seward, and one with myself. Elizabeth's copy differs in being varnished.

25 https://www.gracesguide.co.uk/Thornycroft

26 https://www.iwm.org.uk/collections/item/object/30004029

27 Andrew Hodges, *Alan Turing: The Enigma*, pp.397-8, Vintage, film tie-in edition 2014, first published by Simon and Schuster 1983.

28 See http://www.unithistories.com/officers/RNVR_officersS.htm for Bill's service history.

29 http://www.naval-history.net/xDKEscorts00Index.htm. I am grateful to my cousin Nigel Blanchford for sending me this link.

30 For the full text of this poem see: http://www.harry-tates.org.uk/veteranstales21d.htm.

31 'Navy's 94 Days' Battle to Keep the Channel Open', by Cmdr Kenneth Edwards, RN, *The Daily Telegraph*, 9 September 1944, p.2.

32 Nicholas Monsarrat, *Three Corvettes*, Cassell, 1945; *The Cruel Sea*, Cassell, 1951.

33 https://en.wikipedia.org/wiki/Flower-class_corvette

34 For a full explanation of these measures, see Chapter 3 of Malcolm Llewellyn-Jones, *The Royal Navy and Anti-Submarine Warfare 1917-49*, Routledge, 2006.

35 S.J.Connolly, *op. cit.*, p.225.

36 'Malone Conservation Area Character Appraisal Report', The Planning Service, Department of the Environment Northern Ireland, 2004, pp. 34-7. The report may be downloaded at: https://www.planningni.gov.uk/downloads/conservation-malone-report.pdf

Index

Australia, 76-9

Barton, Harriet, 118, 125-30
'Beech Park', Lurgan, 43-4, 53-4
Belfast,
  and linen, 1-4
  living in, 47, 51, 55
  and the Troubles, 128
Belfast Steamship Company, 129-30
'Belhaven', 51, 61, 121-30
Blanchford, Charlotte ('Lottie') (Seward), 79-86, 97
Blanchford, Hubert, 85-6
Blundell's School, 86, 91, 93-4
Bodine, Eliza Ann, viii, 31-3, 37
Bodine, Mary ('Polly') (Housman), 31-9
Butterfield, William, 5-6

Church of Ireland, 4-6
Clarendon, Desmond, 1, 47-9, 55, 61
Clarendon, Frederick, 10-11
Clarendon, Lavinia (Ewart), 10-19
Clarendon, Nina (Jones), x, 20, 38, 40-53, 57, 121, 126
Clarendon, Rev. Randal, 11-12, 53
Clarendon, Rev. Thomas, 10-19, 52
Clarendon, Victor, CBE, 11-12, 20, 40-1, 51-3, 57-9, 121, 126, 137-9
Coastal Motor Boats (CMBs), ix, 89-90
Convoys, 99-107, 136
'Cromer House', Teddington, 95
'Cromwell Court', Kingston Hill, 118-20
Crosslé, Waller (Jones), 23-4, 43-4

Daly, Neil, 59-60
D-Day, 104-7
Dundela, St Mark's Church, 5-6

Emigrants' Depot, Plymouth, 69-73
Ewart, Gundreda, 7, 9
Ewart, Lady Mary (Heard), 6-7
Ewart, Sir Ivan, 137
Ewart, Sir William, 1st Baronet (1817-89), vii, 1-2, 4-6, 13-17
Ewart, Sir William Quartus, 2nd Baronet (1844-1919), 5-7
Ewart, William (1759-1851), 1
Ewart, William (1789-1873), 1
Ewart, William and Son Limited, 1, 19, 47, 131-2

Far East, naval operations in, 108, 110-16
Finglas(s) Private Mental Home, 27-30
First World War, ix
Fitzroy, Lady, 64-6
Freemasons' Lodge, Negapatam, 83-5

Good Intent, brig, 67-8
Grahame, Winston, 66
Gregory, Anne (Van Treight), 27, 30
Gregory, Richard, 28-30
Gregory, William, 27

Home Front, the, 116-20
Housman, Captain George, 31-7, 39
Housman, Virginia (Dawson), 37
Housman, William Albert, viii, 31, 38-9

India, 79-85
Inver, HMS, 107-18

'J.J.' ('Jack'), 23-7
Jones, Albretta (Housman), 31, 38-9, 49-50
Jones, Emily ('Tatters'), 41-3; *see also* 'Violet'
Jones, Isaac, 20

Jones, Mary (Gregory), 21-2
Jones, Philip, 21
Jones, Philip Howard William, 21, 30-1, 44, 49-50
Jones, Thomas, 20-1, 23
Jubilee, schooner, 68-9, 136

Kidd, Dorothy ('Boo') (Seward), 91, 95, 118

Lewis, C.S., 5-9, 55
Linen, Irish, 1-4, 46
Lisle family, 85
Loosestrife, HMS, 106-7

Magee, Commander Brian, 127
Magee, Virginia (Clarendon), 47-51, 55-9, 61-2, 116
Magheralin ('Maralin'), parish church and rectory, 11, 18-19, 51-2
Malone Road, Belfast, 121-2
McCready, Wyclif, 61-2

Nutgrove School, Rathfarnham, 20-23

Quimper, Brittany, 63-6

Poldark novels, 66
Pulo We (Sabang), Indonesia, 112-14

Rendell, John, 63-6

Sailors' Snug Harbor, 39
Saltarelo, HMS, 99-104
Seward, Charlotte Poe (Renell), 69, 71-4
Seward, Etta (Elliott), 79-86, 97
Seward, Grace (Edwards), 87-8, 94-6, 98, 118-20
Seward, Maureen (Clarendon),
  early childhood in New York and Belfast, 47-51
  schooling, 55-6
  travel in Germany and Italy, 57-9
  wartime in Belfast (1939-42), 59-62, 100, 116
  marriage, 61-2, 102
  early years of marriage (1942-6), 116-18
Seward, Ralph, 79, 84-5, 87
Seward, Samuel Henry, 71-3, 76-9
Seward, William (d.1815), 67-9
Seward, William John (1791-1858), 63, 69-74
Seward, William Rendell (1816-84), 71-6
Seward, William Renell (1845-?), 79-86
Seward, William Renell ('Bill') (1912-66),
  relationship with father, 90-3
  schooling, 55-6, 94
  career at Thornycroft's, 96-8, 115
  war service, 61, 98-116
  marriage, 61-2, 102
  promotion to Lieutenant Commander, RNVR, 107
  birth and early years of first child (Tony), 104, 118-20
Seward, William Thomas Renell (1880-1928), ix, 79, 84-5, 87-93
Sinn Fein, 53-4
South India Railway, 79, 82
Staten Island, New York, 31-9, 47
'Station Wagon', 123-4

Thornycroft, John I. and Co. Ltd, ix, 87-92, 133
Turing, Alan, 95-6

'Violet', 23-7; *see also* Jones, Emily

Watson, Mary (Jones), 23-6, 43-5, 53-4
Webber, Hadassah (Seward), 71-5
Webber, William, 72-3, 75-6
Webber, William John Seward, 73, 75